ORGANIZED LIVING

SHIRA GILL

PHOTOGRAPHY BY VIVIAN JOHNSON

ORGANIZED LIVING

Solutions and Inspiration for Your Home

TEN SPEED PRESS
California | New York

CONTENTS

INTRODUCTION

MY STORY

When people learn that I'm a professional home organizer, they always lean in and ask the same question: "So, is your home *really* that organized?" Spoiler alert: The answer is *yes*.

But here's what I want you to know before we go any further. My need for a streamlined and organized home was not born out of my love for alphabetized file folders or color-coded baskets (although I do appreciate a good basket). I keep my house the way I do because of my deep desire to create order and beauty in a world that often feels fractured and painful.

I grew up in the San Francisco Bay Area, the only child of colorful, creative parents who tried for years to overcome their incompatibilities but finally made the wise decision to end their marriage when I was eight. There was fighting and friction and ultimately a court-appointed joint custody schedule, which required me to shuffle myself, and my things, back and forth from house to house every other day. My father was dynamic, generous, charismatic, and brilliant but also suffered from debilitating bouts of depression and despair. I channeled my childhood anxieties into making my personal space feel good, spending hours alone in my room arranging the things I owned into pleasing vignettes. During those formative years that often felt frightening and painful, organizing my life and surroundings helped me create a sense of peace, order, beauty, and flow. Years later, when I tragically lost my father after a long battle with depression, maintaining an organized home (and helping others do the same) gave me a sense of purpose and helped me move through the crushing waves of grief. Organization became an important form of self-care, a practice I still rely upon to help restore my spirits when I feel the most broken.

Once I had learned how to successfully transform my own space, I volunteered (begged!) to help my friends and family members apply the process to their homes. I was always wildly curious about other people and asked these "clients" a series of questions before diving in: What's important to you right now? How do you want to present yourself to the world? How do you want to *feel* in your space? Next, we would get down to work, letting go of things that didn't serve the vision and neatly arranging the keepers—often repurposing things they already owned such as bins, baskets, art, or textiles. Even my most reluctant friends gasped with delight when I helped them unlock the hidden potential of their spaces, quickly editing and organizing their closets, bedrooms, or workspaces. It felt like magic. I saw firsthand how the process of transforming one's space had the power to propel people toward their bigger goals. I realized that, in addition to improving their living spaces, I was helping them get in touch with their true passions, purpose, and potential—setting them up to be the best version of themselves.

It never occurred to me that my niche hobby could become a career (I had dedicated my life to being an actor in the theater for nearly twenty years), but at eight months pregnant with my first daughter, I lost my full-time event planning job in a wave of company layoffs and was forced to reconsider my plans.

While staying home with my daughter Chloe for nearly a year, I realized that every single parent I knew was completely overwhelmed by clutter and struggling to keep up with the influx of toys, gear, and gadgets that often accompany parenthood. When the women in my new moms group asked how I managed to avoid the clutter trap, I realized that I had unknowingly defined my *less-is-more* home-organizing process and minimalist philosophy. My brand of minimalism confronted excess, waste, and the pressure to consume without limits—without depriving me of the things I loved. I had no business plan, no training whatsoever, truly nothing but a strong desire to help make other people's lives a little easier by sharing the practices that had become second nature to me. So, I threw together a website, sent an email announcing my services to everyone I knew, and set out on a mission to help others reduce physical and mental clutter and create homes that felt good.

Within days of announcing my business, I had booked my first clients. I started off spending the weekdays with Chloe and working in three-hour sessions on Saturdays and Sundays when my husband, Jordan, could be home with her. After years of cobbling jobs together in the theater and hospitality industry, I finally felt I had stumbled onto something I loved that

could have a positive impact, pay the bills, and afford me the luxury of maximizing time with my new daughter. It was thrilling. Each client I met had a new and fascinating set of circumstances and challenges to navigate, which kept the work endlessly stimulating and exciting. I worked with artists, teachers, therapists, physicians, attorneys, tech entrepreneurs, government employees, and even NASA scientists. I helped people who were navigating everything from grief and loss to anxiety, depression, and divorce. I worked in gated mansions that took up entire city blocks and tiny studio apartments in walk-up buildings. Over the course of my lengthy career, I've unearthed firearms, sex toys, precious jewelry, and wads of cash. I've found myself in the middle of marital disputes, temper tantrums, and emotional breakdowns. I've been served caviar and champagne, and I've also been invited to clean up rat droppings, cat urine, and mold. You name it, I've seen it. I've felt honored and humbled that so many people trusted me enough to let me sort through their most treasured (and private) possessions and confide in me. It's been an exhilarating ride.

As my experience grew, I started to see universal themes emerge. Buried under the clutter was shame, guilt, anxiety, depression, and loss. I wanted to help my clients affect change both from the outside in and the inside out, so in 2016 I studied at the Life Coach School and received my coaching certification. I integrated the coaching I'd learned into my organizing sessions, enabling me to go deeper with my clients and give them tools to start processing whatever was at the root of their clutter. After a decade of work in the field, I was able to refine my philosophy into an easy-to-follow five-step process: Clarify, Edit, Organize, Elevate, and Maintain. My first book, *Minimalista,* shares my entire toolkit with readers and breaks down how to use your home as a vehicle to get unstuck, create a home you love, and live the life you want.

I've also expanded my business beyond one-on-one home organizing. To help people at a more accessible price point, I created a suite of online courses that have now been taken by thousands of people all over the world. I also launched a business mentorship program to help other entrepreneurs start and scale their own successful home-organizing and lifestyle businesses.

While my career has evolved to include writing books, speaking, and coaching, organizing spaces is still where I turn to find flow, purpose, and joy. The profession has provided me with the most incredible and deeply

ORGANIZED ENOUGH

There has been some backlash against the consumer-based brand of organizing that's become popular on social media in recent years. Here's the great news: there is absolutely no need to fill your home with matching bins or decant your laundry soap into a pretty glass dispenser unless you actually want to. There is no one-size-fits-all solution for how to organize your home. If color-coding your refrigerator makes you smile, lean in and embrace your rainbow-filled life! If that level of organization prompts a major eye roll, just take a pass.

At the end of the day, the goal of an organized home is to make your life easier and more efficient. Can you organize your home and life without buying new products or setting up a color-coded snack station? Absolutely. Bells and whistles are fully optional.

LIVING WITH LESS: A PEEK INSIDE MY HOME

Since launching my business well over a decade ago, I've used my own home as my creative laboratory—editing, organizing, and styling each space so I could teach my clients my process through actual experience. The 1200-square-foot craftsman bungalow I share with my husband, two daughters, and Australian shepherd, Patches, has been through many transitions. We've opened walls, removed doors from kitchen cabinets, painted every surface, rearranged furniture, tried different systems and products, organized and reorganized. But the thing that's had the single biggest impact? Living with less stuff. The more our family has worked to clarify what's important to us (community, creativity, travel, ice cream), the easier it's been to release the things that were standing in the way. Since our home doesn't have an attic, garage, or even an entry closet, we've had to be very selective about what we fill it with. If we don't love it, need it, or use it with frequency, it goes. Now I get the same thrill I used to get from shopping simply by filling a donation bag. Owning less has improved my life on every level, creating more time, energy, freedom, and spaciousness to focus on the things I value most. If asked to choose between space or stuff, I'd pick space every time.

satisfying career I could imagine. Organizing combines my love for and curiosity about people with my interest in psychology, personal growth, and human development—it includes even my passion for fashion, styling, and design. Teaching others how to create living spaces that look good, feel good, and improve their lives on every level has been one of the greatest joys of my life.

For this book I traveled to interview and tour the homes of twenty-five of the top organizing experts across the globe. While each organizer has their own story and set of skills and talents, they are all united by a shared desire to help people clear clutter, simplify and systematize their spaces, and transform their homes and lives.

The opportunities I've had to explore other organizers' living spaces (both over the course of my career and to produce this book) have left me feeling energized and equipped with an expanded toolkit to incorporate into my work and my own home. With each connection, I realized I was in the unique position of having an all-access pass to gain inspiration and wisdom from the homes of my colleagues. This book is borne out of the desire to give others a peek into this rarely seen world: the very organized homes of people who organize others' homes.

A BRIEF HISTORY OF HOME ORGANIZING

When I started out in 2010 and people asked what I did for work, the term "professional home organizer" was often met with blank stares and shrugs that suggested, *Well, I guess anything is possible*. I didn't know a single person who shared my niche career, but with a little research I discovered a small but thriving organization, the National Association for Productivity and Organizing Professionals. NAPO was founded by a small group of women in Los Angeles in 1985 with the goal of providing education, enhancing business connections, advancing industry research, and increasing public awareness of the profession.

In recent years, the world of professional organizing has exploded. Through books, TV shows, and the arrival of the first globally recognized celebrity home organizer, Marie Kondo, home organizers have been elevated to thought leaders and lifestyle influencers. Home organizers have further cemented their place in the cultural zeitgeist through content channels such as blogs and podcasts, and social media platforms including Instagram and TikTok. NAPO has now grown to include thirty local chapters made up of over four thousand members spanning the globe. The National Association of Black Professional Organizers (NABPO) was founded in 2017 to provide education and support to professional organizers of all ethnic backgrounds, and January has been officially declared "Get Organized Month."

The Container Store, a US-based retail chain specializing in home-organizing products and custom closets, has grown into an empire with nearly one hundred locations across the nation. The industry has expanded to include training and certification programs, summits, conferences, courses, and retreats. In addition, with a quick Google search, you can now find organizers who specialize in everything under the sun, including ADHD, digital organizing (such as email and photo management), downsizing and moves, spatial planning, and sustainability. You name it, there's an organizing expert ready to help.

HOW DID WE GET HERE?

Overconsumption (particularly in the United States) has become so rampant that an entire community of professionals has emerged who are dedicated to helping people cut clutter and live more intentionally and sustainably. The field of home organization is predicated on a culture that has acquired more than it can keep up with.

It's never been easier to order housewares, clothes, or electronics with the click of a button. But the excess we've accumulated has resulted in a whole host of problems including consumer debt, overstuffed homes, physical and mental stress, and a landfill crisis. Our collective mass consumption has led us to a tipping point where our possessions may feel more overwhelming and stifling than liberating. I can't tell you how many of my clients have shared that it would be a tremendous relief if their entire garage or basement vanished in a fire or other natural disaster. "Can you just torch the whole thing, so I don't have to deal with it?" While we certainly didn't need a global pandemic to teach us that our homes shape our lives, our new circumstances have prompted people all over the world to evaluate the state of their homes and reassess how they want to live.

BLACK GIRLS WHO ORGANIZE

In researching this book, I met so many organizers who are continuing to broaden and evolve the industry. One example is Dalys Macon, the founder of the organizing consultancy D'Vine Order. She is a breast cancer survivor and a government contractor with thirty-eight years of service including four years of military service. Her path to becoming a professional home organizer started with taking one of the early NAPO classes to learn about the industry. Dalys had always been exceptionally tidy, but it took her thirteen years of organizing for friends and family before she took the leap and launched her business in 2019.

An avid reader of industry books, magazines, and blogs, Dalys found a huge gap in the organizing industry when it came to whose voices were being elevated in the press or media. She decided it was up to her to create a platform that would spotlight women of color in the industry. Dalys started reaching out to other organizers of color to connect and share resources, and soon after, in January 2020, she officially launched Black Girls Who Organize (BGWO). The platform started as an Instagram account with the goal of highlighting one woman of color each month for a full year, but the community grew so fast that Dalys ended up featuring more than seventy women over those first twelve months. She currently has an eight-month waitlist to be featured on the platform. In addition to the Instagram community, BGWO also hosts monthly meetings with speakers, skill sharing, and the popular "What's on Your Mind" segment, where new organizers can ask how to handle everything from contracts to rates to best business practices. Women from London, Nigeria, and Ghana have joined the community, and Dalys plans to launch retreats and teaching summits in the future to further empower and support the thriving, diverse community of organizers she has built. She is beloved among clients and colleagues alike and has singlehandedly made an important and powerful impact on the organizing industry.

5 REASONS TO GET ORGANIZED NOW

EFFICIENCY | Rather than spending twenty minutes searching frantically for your wallet, keys, pens, or umbrella, imagine reclaiming that time for far more valuable pursuits.

CLARITY AND CONTROL | When every item in your living space serves a purpose and has a clearly designated home, you can confidently locate whatever you need within seconds and enable family members to do the same. Oh joy!

FREEDOM | Want to rent out your home, pack up for a weekend getaway, or host a party at a moment's notice without frantically tidying? An organized home helps facilitate whatever activities you want to do with ease.

TRANQUILITY | At the most basic level, organization equates to mental peace. When you streamline and organize your belongings, there is a ripple effect that improves every single aspect of your life. Once more, with feeling: Every. Single. Aspect.

SUSTAINABILITY | An organized home makes it easier to reduce waste and stop overbuying. We're at a critical point of overconsumption, but it's not too late to shift our behaviors and lighten our environmental footprint.

WHY I WROTE THIS BOOK

While I may have felt alone when I started my organizing career, the power of the internet and social media has enabled me to connect with fellow organizers across the globe, including cities as far away as Sydney, Tel Aviv, Manila, and Mexico City. I've had the great pleasure of getting to know these colleagues (either virtually or in person) and of being invited into their homes. Whenever I've had the occasion to, I've asked my colleagues how they organize and optimize their own spaces. "Where do you store your laundry hamper? What's under your kitchen sink? How many sets of sheets do you have? What do you do with the annoying tiny plastic things your kids bring home from birthday parties?"

If you're the type of person who has wondered about the inside of an organizer's home, chances are you've also asked the other most frequent question I get: "Why did you become an organizer?" As my colleagues have become my close friends, I've learned that while we've all arrived in the same profession, our paths have varied widely. There is a common misconception that we are driven by a shared love of file folders and an affinity for stacks of matching, plastic bins. Here's the deeper truth: home organization is human-centered work, and we not only transform our clients' living spaces but often their lives, too. While most of us appreciate a row of neatly labeled bins, what unites us and fuels our work is a desire to help create order, ease, beauty, and flow and help improve other people's lives on every level. Many of us have gravitated to this transformational work because of our own trauma or grief, including difficult childhoods, divorce, or loss. We have deep empathy and a desire to help. Creating order and implementing functional systems are how we achieve these ends.

This book will introduce you not only to the aspirational spaces of the most organized people in the world, but also to the organizers themselves and to the passion that fuels their work. We'll travel around the globe visiting the homes of minimalists living in three-hundred-square-foot apartments (and even one Airstream trailer!), maximalists in sprawling suburban homes, and everything in between. You'll meet niche organizers who've dedicated their careers to a single type of space, and you'll meet others who love the challenge of organizing an entire home. You'll be introduced to organizers who launched their businesses after established careers as attorneys, marine biologists, and nurses, and others who started fresh out of school in the midst of

a worldwide pandemic. Through images and interviews, you'll be treated to eye candy and interior inspiration, as well as gain expert tips, resources, and clever organizing strategies you can apply to your own home.

I personally visited with each one of these experts, traveling around the world with my longtime collaborator, Vivian Johnson, who captured every image in this book. We did not bring a team of stylists or a suitcase full of props, so the homes you'll see ahead are the real deal and a reflection of how these professional organizers actually live. Hop around, choose your own adventure, and get ready for some fun.

The twenty-five experts profiled in this book have opened their homes, cabinets, and drawers (so brave!) so that you can see what resonates and cherry-pick what works for you. I've also provided organizing "cheat sheets" throughout the book so you can refer to tips by category (these include Let's Get Sustainable, Small Space Solutions, Living with Kids, and Working from Home). Get cozy, make yourself at home, and let's get to it. I can't wait to introduce you to the talented, dynamic, and diverse group of people I'm lucky to call my colleagues and friends. Let's meet the organizers . . .

Ready to organize your home and life but wondering what you need to get started? Before you run out to buy every gadget, gizmo, and tool in sight . . . don't! I've rounded up a simple starter kit to help you edit and organize like a pro. These are the tools of the trade that organizing professionals use most. Let's go!

BOXES AND BINS AND BAGS, OH MY

It's crucial to have some sturdy vessels on hand as you organize, so you can easily pack up trash, recycling, compostables, donations, and even the items you want to sell, return, or hand off. For most projects, a stack of paper grocery bags will do the trick. However, if you're dealing with heavy or bulky items, lawn and leaf bags, bankers boxes, or those massive blue totes from IKEA (did somebody say "FRAKTA"!?) will do the trick.

DESTINATION SIGNS

Decluttering a home can be a messy business, and it can be easy to lose track of what goes where. Using sticky notes or printable signs will create a helpful visual cue so you can keep the piles straight. Typical categories include keep, donate, consign, give to a friend, trash, recycle, compost, shred, return, repair, and relocate.

A "TRANSITIONAL" BIN

While organizing and decluttering, there are sure to be items that need to be relocated to other rooms. Instead of relocating each item as you encounter it, stow the items that need to be relocated in a "transitional" bin so you can return them all at once when you're ready. Any oversize bin, basket, or tote bag will do the trick here.

A TAPE MEASURE

Your run-of-the-mill hardware store tape measure is about to become your BFF. Organizers rely on this simple tool to help measure drawers, cabinets, and shelves so they can be sure to buy the right organizing products. A tape measure can also come in handy if you want to rearrange a room or swap furniture.

STICKY STUFF

Museum gel or sticky putty dots are must-haves for keeping everything from art to drawer organizers in place. Adhering one of these adhesives to the back corners of your drawer dividers will prevent slippage. Goo Gone or the natural alternative lemon oil are favorites for safely removing the residue left behind from stickers, labels, or decals. Sticky notes are indispensable for jotting down notes and keeping the piles in order.

A NOTE-TAKING DEVICE

Most organizers I know rely on a note-taking app on their phones for jotting down project-related notes such as dimensions, measurements, and shopping lists, but a notepad and pen will get the job done.

A LABEL MAKER

Many pros favor the industry leaders Cricut or P-touch labelers, or opt to order custom sticker labels, but you can keep it casual and use a chalk pen, a Wine Glass Writer pen (rubs right off), or a good old-fashioned marker of your choice

(Sharpies are a go-to for most) paired with masking tape, painter's tape, or washi tape in the color of your choice.

CORD TIE ORGANIZERS

A common organizing pet peeve is cord chaos! Keep your cords tidy by using nylon cable zip ties, Velcro strips, rubber twist ties, or even magnetic cable ties. Extra credit if you want to add cord tags or handwritten labels so you never lose track of which cord goes to what device. PSA: A cable box makes it easy to tuck away that pesky jumble of cords behind your desk neatly and out of sight.

CLEANING SUPPLIES

Obvious as it may seem, it's worth noting that having a bottle of all-purpose cleaner and a handful of rags is sure to come in handy while you're organizing. You may want to keep a broom or vacuum within reach as well.

SNACKS

Organizing is hard work. Treat yourself to some of your favorite savory or sweet goodies to boost your mood and give you more stamina.

OTHER PRO FAVORITES

Many of the experts I interviewed cited label scrapers, pliers, hammers, shims, batteries, twine, folding boards, and Elfa wrenches as handy tools. And remember, most experts agree that the best practice for buying containers and organizing products is *after* decluttering and "shopping" your own home for supplies you might already own so you can ensure you only buy what you need. Make sure to measure the height, width, and depth of the space you're organizing, and jot down a list and a plan before you shop so you can avoid buyer's remorse—and avoid adding more clutter to your space.

HOME TOURS

TINKA MARKHAM PIPER

COLORFUL AND CREATIVE IN MONTREAL

TINKA'S STORY

Tinka had a dynamic and nomadic childhood. The daughter of a foreign news correspondent, she lived in seven countries in a span of fourteen years. As a young child, she and her family were evacuated from war zones in Saigon, Vietnam, and Beirut, Lebanon. Her parents instilled the value of "bloom where you're planted" so that amid the constant upheaval, she was always curious about new places, people, and experiences. Tinka found comfort in making to-do lists and organizing her worldly treasures and loved creating a nest wherever she went, from her own bedroom to friends' spaces. She was even found at a friend's sleepover organizing the family bathroom supplies! Much to the chagrin of her younger brother, she created her own Dewey Decimal library. If he wanted to borrow a book, he had to fill out a slip and be on the hook for late fees.

When Tinka lost her father suddenly as a teenager, she poured her energy and ambition into academics, including an undergraduate degree and a teaching credential from Princeton University, and graduate degrees in social work and public health from Columbia University. She credits her close-knit relationships with her family and friends for navigating loss and building resiliency.

In her early career, Tinka pursued a range of professional paths, from working in education reform for AmeriCorps in San Francisco to creating suicide prevention programs in New York City to working as a client advocate and social worker at a public defender's office. After being part of the 9/11 relief efforts with the American Red Cross and FEMA, Tinka found a dream job in research, working at an urban epidemiology institute where she oversaw a project at a New York City morgue that evaluated suicides, homicides, and overdoses. She mentions all of this casually like it is *no big deal*.

After moving to Montreal, Canada, with her husband (her high school and college sweetheart), Tinka worked at McGill University in global health and social policy until she finally sought out what she loved most: finding creative solutions to people's living spaces, which would in turn change their emotional health for the better. Her itinerant childhood had given her the nesting tools to transform any space into an instant home. By combining her clinical social-work skills with her public-health training, she realized she could create a business that united her love of decluttering, organizing, and

redesigning. Her business Solve My Space was formed in 2012 with a desire for "making home feel good."

A self-described chaos counselor and space solver, Tinka brilliantly merges her background in mental health with her passion for organization and design. Her motto is "keep it light but go deep," and she's always looking for new ways to help people bridge the gap between improving the state of their home and their mental health. Her boutique organizing business is known for helping people navigate big life transitions with thoughtful, feel-good makeovers, all the while teaching them concrete tools. During the pandemic lockdown, Tinka volunteered her services virtually, helping more than one hundred people all over the globe to overhaul their spaces and adjust to the new work- and school-from-home situations that were causing anxiety and unrest. She also launched her popular "Ask Tinka" home advice column,

where she counsels readers on everything from how to get their donations out the door to how to brighten a home during the dreary winter months.

Mental health remains the driving force of Tinka's work. She believes that addressing the emotional issues around home are essential to organizing our most intimate spaces. She frequently works with clients both in-home and remotely who are navigating relationship stress, anxiety, depression, ADHD, grief, or loss. Tinka brings joy, humor, vulnerability, and a generosity of spirit to everything she does. In her bright, cheery home and the spaces she's transformed all over the world, you can see the invisible hand of Tinka's magic touch.

TINKA'S HOME

Warning: Entering Tinka's home for the first time may prompt squeals of delight. The colorful and spacious home is a feast for the eyes, with modern architecture, high ceilings, and things to explore and revel in. She jokes that she's a bit of a maximalist, a collector who loves to surround herself with art, books, textiles, ceramics, and vintage treasures. She's a huge fan of the Australian artist Rachel Castle, showcasing her work throughout her house in the form of tea towels (elevated in frames), bedding, pillows, and original artwork. Tinka also loves supporting local and emerging artists (such as Ara Osterweil, Nova Mercury, Judit Just, Alexandra Collin, and Véronique Buist), and the pieces she owns are thoughtfully curated and lovingly displayed. Her space is punctuated with stars, circles, ovals, and round, soft shapes in contrasting colors, creating a sense of childlike wonder and whimsy. It feels like there's a little wink around each corner.

To balance her desire to collect with her husband's more minimalist tendencies, she and Andrew had custom floor-to-ceiling built-ins made to line the walls of the main floor. The cabinets have ample room to store Tinka's extensive art and office supplies, seasonal treasures, and memorabilia, but everything magically disappears when the doors are closed, creating a clean, minimal aesthetic. The kitchen island resembles a massive dining table and has more clever concealed storage built in below, perfect for stowing Tinka's beloved platters, vases, candles, crockpots, serving dishes, place mats, and collectables. Andrew, a professor of digital humanities at McGill, also has a sharp eye for aesthetics, as evidenced by his stylish (and immaculate) home

office furnished with art and books neatly organized by both language and subject. Tinka has taken the lead on decorating the home with her signature and playful more-is-more style, while Andrew has led the architectural and design decisions (opting for a sleek, minimal aesthetic), proving that it is possible for maximalists and minimalists to successfully collaborate and cohabitate. No small victory!

With two teenagers in the house, Tinka has created several smart systems to help her kids clean up independently. A "teen clean-up kit" lives in the laundry room and includes a cordless mini vacuum, all-purpose cleaner, patterned cleaning rags, and a room aromatherapy spray. On the kitchen counters, a basket tray dubbed the "crap collector" serves as a convenient drop zone for all the miscellaneous items found around the house. At the end of the week, Tinka empties the basket onto the dining table, and everything is relocated or donated (if not claimed).

I am struck by how bold and cheery the utilitarian spaces are throughout the home. There's the tiny half bath with playful art vertically lining the walls, accented with bright flowers and a candle perched on a tiny ledge. The entry is furnished with bright, welcoming art, plants, plug-in lights, and a bright woven pink-and-fuchsia mat beneath the snow boots. Office supplies and stationery are stored in stacks of neon boxes instead of the dismal alternatives from the office supply store. The kitchen pantry features snacks and cooking staples organized into pastel bins that sit beneath an artful arrangement of boldly colored ceramics, trays, cookie jars, and vases. Even the laundry room, typically known for being a drab, functional area, is adorned floor to ceiling with colorful art, decor, and pom-poms, making it a cheerful and inviting space that makes dreaded household chores ever more inviting.

Montreal has dramatic seasonal shifts, and Tinka loves to mark the changing seasons with small, visual celebrations for each transition. She swaps out art, platters, centerpieces, and plants, and even rotates ceramics, felt objects, tassels, garlands, fruit, and flowers depending on the time of year. When I visit on a cool October day, I'm greeted by a fire burning in the living room, poutine from Tinka's favorite local spot to warm us up, and the most delightful display of mini pumpkins and seasonal decor accenting each room—a true celebration of autumn! Even though this colorful, maximalist haven couldn't be more different from my own home, I consider sending for my things.

Our homes and environments are not just boxes to eat, sleep, and work in. They can help dramatically shift our moods and alter how we feel on a day-to-day basis. Even spending a single day in Tinka's home, full of beads, tassels, pom-poms, stacked stools, playhouses, paper cutouts, and ceramics, felt transformative and inspiring. At one point, I called my husband and declared we needed more art and pom-poms in our home. I could practically feel him rolling his eyes, but no matter. The space, like Tinka herself, can't help but lift your spirits and make you smile.

TIPS + TAKEAWAYS

· Add pops of color and joyful touches such as art, plants, and textiles to the utilitarian areas of your home, like the laundry room, entry, and food pantry.

· Mark and celebrate the seasons with visual cues. Swap out not just linens, but also art, objects, and textiles, using a seasonal display shelf like Tinka (who even moves furniture around).

· Frame a tea towel or textile as a budget-friendly way to showcase an artist you love.

· Add extra storage space throughout your home with art ledges. They're perfect for storing spices in the kitchen, toiletries in the bathroom, plants and decorative objects in bedrooms and hallways, and they're also a clever way to display framed art without damaging the walls.

· When choosing storage vessels, think outside the box (I couldn't help myself!). Employ playful shapes. Circles, ovals, stars, and round spheres create a soft touch and a sense of childlike whimsy.

· Bring on the fairy lights, candles, and other ambient illuminating sources during the darker winter months. Brighten up your space and boost your spirits with pops of color and lighter textiles and greenery.

Q/A WITH TINKA MARKHAM PIPER

WHAT MIGHT PEOPLE BE SURPRISED TO LEARN ABOUT YOU?

I'm a colorful, sentimental maximalist with lots of collections. Minimalism is not really part of my vocabulary! I've lived in eight countries and speak four languages. I had a career in social work and public health before I started my own business.

FAVORITE SPACE TO ORGANIZE?

The messiest, most intense, most upside-down spaces. I like the extra-challenging jobs that feel overwhelming, but I know there are solutions that will completely transform the spaces, so my client feels *WOW!*

DIRTY LITTLE CLUTTER SECRET?

I stuff a ton of things into our front hall closet (much to the despair of my patient family). I also use our car as a dumping ground for projects, donations, and client items (also much to the annoyance of my family).

CAN'T-LIVE-WITHOUT ORGANIZING TOOL?

A sense of humor.

WHAT'S IN YOUR ORGANIZING TOOLKIT?

Dark chocolate, instant coffee, measuring tape, sticky notes, label maker, Sharpies, transparent boxes filled with all the supplies (scissors, Magic Eraser, binder clips, batteries, cute labels), Kleenex (sometimes it's needed), and brown paper lawn bags for donations. Also, an aromatherapy "no stress" spray when we need some motivation, focus, or calm. It reminds us to pause for a bit, take stock of where we are, and re-energize our efforts to keep on going.

WHAT DO YOU DO WHEN YOU FEEL OVERWHELMED IN A HOME OR SPACE?

I figure out why I'm overwhelmed and what's making me go "AAARGGH!" I usually take a break, get some coffee and chocolate, and reboot with simple and small steps. Just tackle each problem "bird by bird!" (as the author Anne Lamott says).

MOST COMMON MISCONCEPTION ABOUT PRO ORGANIZERS?

That we are all type-A personalities with impeccable homes and children, who are also organized and clean their rooms. Nope!

WHEN YOU'RE NOT ORGANIZING, YOU'RE PROBABLY . . .

Connecting with family and friends, moving furniture around at home, trying to convince my kids to switch up their rooms (again), researching cool artists, browsing vintage stores, avoiding exercise, and eating chocolate.

GO-TO DAILY UNIFORM?

Tunic, leggings, my Soludos rainbow sneakers. Lots of stripes and pops of color. I love wearing kids' clothes, too, because they are just way more fun.

A RISK YOU TOOK THAT PAID OFF?

Realizing that I was on a career path that looked right but didn't feel right. Having the support of my husband, family, and friends to step off that path and start something completely different that felt right. Solve my space, baby!

ACTUAL MORNING ROUTINE?

Coffee, coffee, coffee. Stretching. Mother hen moments with my exasperating yet awesome teenagers. I can't leave the house without a shower, a made bed, and a tidy kitchen.

ACTUAL EVENING ROUTINE?

Family shenanigans with two teenagers, my husband, and everyone's favorite family member, Syd (our dog). Calling my mom (I'm her "helicopter daughter" because I call All. The. Time.). Making a to-do list for the next day. Going to bed too late and making another resolution to try again tomorrow.

THE PARISIAN ESSENTIALIST

MARIE'S STORY

Sometimes the things that make us appear different or strange end up being our greatest assets. Such was the case with Marie, whose lifelong passion for beauty and order often came across as peculiar, eccentric, or even obsessive to others.

Born and raised in Paris, she was always acutely aware of her surroundings and environment, often spending hours editing, sorting, and arranging her belongings. A nature lover from birth, she adored escaping the city to visit her grandmother in a small village where she could climb trees, take walks in nature, and learn about birds. She recalls "tidying" the stream, removing fallen branches, taking inventory, and arranging the things she found on her path.

While Marie excelled academically, she could often be caught daydreaming and drawing. Fascinated by the origin and evolution of early humans, Marie studied biology, science, and biochemistry with the dream of becoming a paleoanthropologist. After receiving a biology degree and an agricultural engineering degree, she realized that a career in paleoanthropology would require years more of study and travel—a lifestyle that was at odds with her goal of starting a family. She decided to shift gears and obtained her third degree, this time in marketing and business. Marketing appealed to her because it was strategic, process-oriented, and highly visual. Marie excelled in her role overseeing brand identity for large companies and creative agencies but also started feeling a lack of alignment when it came to her work. A passionate advocate for the environment (she married an impact investor with similar values), Marie yearned to find a way to help reduce overconsumption and make a positive impact on the planet. She identified distinct strategies that could be used to shift and rebalance our relationship with our belongings and surroundings and realized that if we held strict and specific standards for the things we consume, we could at the same time reduce visual, mental, and environmental pollution while creating a more harmonious and balanced home and life. She identified three criteria that all personal belongings should meet: beautiful, practical, and sustainable. Marie was able to build an entire process and philosophy around this singular idea, and Interior Ecology was born. For the first time in her life, her passion for beauty and order didn't feel like a flaw or an eccentricity,

it felt like an asset. In 2019 she launched a brand and consulting firm called L'ARRANGEUSE (a combination of the words *improve* and *tidy* in French) to teach others how to transform their homes and lives using her protocol and methodology.

While juggling a full-time job and raising two young kids, she also launched an Instagram platform to demonstrate her process and philosophy, using her own home as an example. Strangers around the world were attracted to her beautiful, organized aesthetic, and the colleagues who were once perplexed by her picture-perfect desk started asking for help with their own spaces. She began offering Zoom consults, businesses asked her to do in-person workshops, and brands asked her to speak at their conferences. COVID-19 only intensified the demand, as people felt the strain of being stuck at home and smothered by the weight and volume of their belongings.

Marie has been able to fully integrate her passion for science and environmentalism with her talent for creating beautiful, functional spaces, modeling and promoting a lifestyle that is both inspiring and environmentally responsible. "I don't help people to tidy their space, I help them change their relationship with the things they own."

On the horizon: a book (*L'Écologie d'Intérieur: Vivre Mieux avec Moins*), a course, and more inspiration on her popular Instagram feed. With a goal of countering the more-is-more culture and ethos, Marie is on a mission to make the sustainable desirable and inspire others to do the same. For this passionate influencer and entrepreneur, Interior Ecology is not just a career path, it's a way of life.

MARIE'S HOME

Marie's home is situated in a bustling and beautiful Parisian neighborhood in a historic building just across the street from the world-famous Bon Marché (sure, I'm jealous, it's fine). At first glance it would seem impossible that the sleek, white, 645-square-foot space Marie calls home is shared with her husband, two children, and even a rescue cat she found in a nearby park. "Where are all of your things?" I blurt out after scanning the living spaces in search of a single cord, appliance, or household item. Marie doesn't consider herself a minimalist (a term she associates with deprivation) but instead an essentialist. With the flourish of a seasoned magician, Marie starts flipping open the sleek, white cabinets that line each wall to reveal all of her family's essentials: a coat closet; a linen cabinet; storage for papers, mementos, clothes, books, and toys; a stocked pantry and refrigerator; a full set of dishes, glassware, pots and pans, and cooking utensils; tools; appliances; and even an oven and microwave (there were uncontrolled, audible gasps at each reveal). Almost everything that the family owns is concealed behind these tall cabinet doors that blend into the walls—even the cooktop is white, so it disappears into the bright white lacquered countertop. Marie admits that critics may call the space stark or clinical, but friends and visitors always mention how calm and at ease they feel in the space—a feature that was completely by design. Marie personally created every detail of her home in collaboration with architect Clémence Murat using principles of Interior Ecology so that the tiny home could be functional, beautiful, and durable. The design duo wanted to respect the historic details of the building while minimizing what Marie refers to as "visual pollution," creating a home that feels surprisingly airy and spacious given the small size. The clean lines and neutral tones result in spaces that are completely free from distraction, with nothing to interrupt the flow or distract the viewer's eye.

While there is no visible entry room or closet, a tall white cabinet pops open with a gentle press to reveal the family's hanging coats, with a shelf for water bottles above and a deep bin for shoes below. The kids place their backpacks inside when they arrive home from school. Across from the entry system is a simple wooden desk with two shallow drawers containing grab-and-go essentials, including wallets, keys, hand sanitizer, a shoehorn, pens, and note paper. The adjacent drawer contains Marie's home office supplies, including her simple and practical filing system consisting of just three folders labeled To Do, To File, and Follow-Ups. Papers are kept to a bare minimum, and when I ask about photos and memorabilia, Marie shows me two small boxes filled with family photos and mementos from her wedding and from each child's baptism. Some of her most precious items are worn daily on her body, including beautiful earrings from her mother and an actual antique nail from an excavation that she uses to keep her perfect bun intact on the top of her head (don't worry, I got a demo).

Despite the small footprint of her home, Marie managed to make space for a designated dining room with a solid wood table she designed and paired with Hans Wegner chairs. Lining the dining room walls, more

concealed storage includes a closet for her husband, Gautier, which he keeps immaculately organized, and a linen closet that has stackable drawers for paperwork and mementos. A small laundry closet holds labeled bins to separate lights, darks, delicates, and items to iron—a brilliant system that has eliminated the need for separate laundry hampers throughout the home.

Cleaning supplies, clothes pins, laundry soap, tools, and even cat litter are contained in clear and enamel jars and canisters, making these utilitarian items stylish and beautiful. Marie owns only a handful of beauty products, which are stored in a single pouch and include blush, mascara, concealer, cream, serum, makeup remover, and a natural deodorant stone which looks lovely on display.

One of the most charming details in the home is the mini cat door that was carved into the hallway. It leads to a hidden nook in the bathroom, so the litter box is both accessible and concealed. Mini ramekins for food and water are displayed in the hallway on a single white tile.

Marie's two children share a room so small it's not even technically considered a bedroom by French real-estate standards. Despite the size, Marie has designed an enchanting wall-to-wall sleep loft (the siblings sleep toe to toe) with a removable ladder and a slim desk for art, homework, and projects. Toys, books, and clothes are stored in the narrow cabinets that line the wall across from the bed, and whimsical, modern cloud sculptures (by Italian company Magis) hang from the ceiling, making the bedroom a perfect space to play, daydream, and rest. Marie prefers to keep their room free from clutter and opts to give and receive edible or experiential gifts to prevent any accumulation of goods. For a recent birthday party, handmade favors were given out: candy-stuffed paper envelopes with a single white balloon adhered to each one—a crowd pleaser with almost zero waste.

It occurs to me that every single object in the apartment (from tools to toys to beauty products) is fully aligned with Marie's mission to invest only in products that are beautiful, practical, and durable. When I ask her how she got her kids and husband on board with this very intentional lifestyle, she shrugs and says it wasn't hard to do. "Life is just easier this way."

TIPS + TAKEAWAYS

· Looking to cut the clutter in your home? Ask for experiential or consumable gifts such as museum passes, theater tickets, a home-cooked meal, or breakfast in bed.

· Use tall cabinets or bookcases with doors (IKEA has affordable options) to minimize "visual pollution" and tuck away household essentials.

· Elevate the utilitarian spaces in your home (closets, laundry room, hallways) by adding art, objects, dried florals, or scented room spray.

· Try this budget hack: instead of installing a towel rack or hook, use a binder clip to secure a hand towel to the edge of your sink (this works for narrow sinks).

· Nest suitcases like Matryoshka dolls inside of one large trunk and use as a coffee table or display, like art. Marie stores all her family's luggage inside a single vintage Louis Vuitton suitcase, which can be tucked under the coffee table in the living room—a stylish and simple storage solution for those tight on space.

· Commit to a cohesive color palette for your home. Marie makes her small space look airy and spacious by using white paint, white countertops, white cabinets accented with pops of pale pink, and wooden furniture.

Q/A WITH MARIE QUÉRU

BIGGEST HOME-ORGANIZING CHALLENGE?

None! As I have been organized since I was very little, I never really had to organize my own home! But in Paris, real estate is quite expensive, especially in my area, so I had to be very creative when it came to conceiving a nice place for four people and a cat in only 60 square meters (645 square feet).

WHAT ARE YOU MOST PROUD OF?

My Interior Ecology concept and protocol. I couldn't imagine just two years ago that I would be talking about this today and receiving so much support for what I do.

FAVORITE SPACE TO ORGANIZE?

Any place as long as there is progress! What I truly love is to see the before and after and how I improve things. I know L'ARRANGEUSE is not easy to pronounce in English, but it comes from "to arrange" that means both "to fix" and "to tidy" in French. My thing is really to arrange the world.

CAN'T-LIVE-WITHOUT ORGANIZING PRODUCT?

My phone! I don't really think there is a "no miss" organizing tool because I truly believe answers are not found in organizing but in changing the relationship to objects. But yes, I couldn't live without my phone as a personal assistant.

MOST TREASURED POSSESSION?

It's not something I possess but something I built: the love I share with my husband. I couldn't live without his love or him.

FAVORITE ORGANIZING TIP OR IDEA?

My five rules of organizing are: make it categorized, visible, accessible, contained, and vertical.

WHAT DO YOU DO WHEN YOU FEEL OVERWHELMED IN A HOME OR SPACE?

I remember that objects don't reproduce themselves, it will come to an end, and then I sub-categorize the job. I had a previous boss who used to say, "Treat problems like sausages, slice by slice."

MOST COMMON MISCONCEPTION ABOUT PRO ORGANIZERS?

We are here to help tidy. For me, we are here to help change the relationship to objects and to consumption.

YOUR DEFINITION OF ORGANIZED?

Someone who is very sensitive to visual, mental, and environmental pollution.

BIGGEST TAKEAWAY OR LESSON LEARNED FROM ORGANIZING OTHER PEOPLE'S HOMES?

We need to change the way we consume in this world. Our consumption is not making us happy, and it is not building a safe future for our children.

ACTUAL MORNING ROUTINE?

Open the window and make my bed, done!

ACTUAL EVENING ROUTINE?

Having a matcha latte and cuddling my cat.

ONE SELF-CARE TIP YOU FOLLOW?

I do everything following my mantra: "Is this beautiful, practical, and durable?"

THE MOST VALUABLE CAREER ADVICE YOU'VE EVER BEEN GIVEN?

"Nothing is irreversible except death."

WHAT KIND OF PLANNER DO YOU USE? HOW DO YOU ORGANIZE YOUR DAY?

I use one from Bookbinders because I find it beautiful, but I don't really need it as I do everything on my phone. I take a moment in the morning to set priorities and start with the hardest task.

GO-TO DAILY UNIFORM?

Anything that is beige, light, and simple in its lines.

NIKKI BOYD

SOUTHERN HOSPITALITY IN CHARLESTON

NIKKI'S STORY

Nikki grew up in a military family and spent her childhood moving between South Carolina, Georgia, Alaska, and Germany. While the nomadic lifestyle had its challenges, Nikki now sees it as a blessing. She became resilient and adaptable, met people from all over the world, and gained insight about other cultures and perspectives. Going to prom in a castle in Germany didn't hurt either.

Nikki's mother taught her how to fold sheets and towels and enrolled her in classes on how to host and entertain, but Nikki didn't learn how to maintain an organized home until she had one of her own. Her husband, Mike, was in the Air Force, which meant that they often had to move at the drop of a hat. Nikki learned how to become a near-professional packer (the moving services loved her) and prided herself on efficiently packing up the entire home and setting up a new one with lightning speed. With three children between them, Nikki made it her mission to create a comfortable and beautiful home so her family could feel at ease whenever and wherever they moved.

Her adaptable nature served her well since she had to transition careers with each move, including jobs as a social service worker for the government, a human resources manager, a school registrar, and even an art framer.

After twenty-four years of service in the military, Mike retired and the couple moved back to Charleston, South Carolina, to start a new phase of life together as empty nesters. Mike encouraged Nikki to pursue her own passions, saying, "You've supported me for my entire career. Now it's your turn to do whatever you want." Nikki didn't yet have a specific dream or goal and laughs recalling how she contemplated sitting on the couch eating Snickers all day. She remembered a girlfriend in England who had shared crafting videos on YouTube, so she decided to film herself organizing and decorating her new home. Always one to love sharing ideas and resources with others, Nikki was thrilled when she started receiving fan mail and thank-you messages from strangers across the globe. She continued sharing content on a range of home projects, including making a lamp out of teacups, setting up a linen closet, and organizing paperwork. What started out as a fun hobby evolved within a few years into a full-blown business. Nikki was able to monetize her videos with ads, affiliate links, and brand partnerships. With the success of her video content, Nikki began taking one-on-one

clients, both in-person and online. Her fanbase mainly consisted of moms who were struggling, as well as empty nesters who felt they could finally invest in having the home of their dreams.

Nikki has loved providing her clients and fans with creative new tools to make their lives easier. She has designed an entire suite of products to help organize everything under the sun, including a digital desktop organizer, and a full stationery line consisting of daily to-do lists, meal planners, cleaning and home maintenance checklists, budgeting planners, and her popular "day on a page" one-sheet planner.

After years of sharing content on how to create a beautifully organized home, Nikki realized she was ready to compile all her material into a set of resources: *Beautifully Organized* (a comprehensive roundup of her best tools), a linen-bound companion workbook, and *Beautifully Organized at Work* (focused on boosting productivity and efficiency in the workplace). For those keeping score at home, that's three books in three years. With so many balls in the air, Nikki has expanded her team to include employees who oversee social

media, video editing, and graphic design, and others who support her on organizing projects, workshops, and speaking engagements. She loves to give back to her community, hiring other military spouses and providing product discounts to military families. In addition, she's recently launched a nonprofit (www.beautifullyorganized.org) to teach kids and families essential life skills that aren't taught in school. Nikki and her team instruct on everything from doing laundry to managing leases to opening a bank account. I'm pretty sure we all need this, or at least I do. While her career shows no signs of slowing down, she does schedule a one- to two-week vacation every quarter so she can minimize burnout and return to work feeling energized and inspired.

What started as a small passion project has evolved into a wildly successful and multifaceted business. With three books, a full product line, an organizing consultancy, and video tutorials that consistently reach millions of viewers on YouTube, Nikki is an inspiring example of what's possible. In just five years, she has created an empire that inspires people to live a beautifully organized life. "This is not just a business for me, it's a calling."

NIKKI'S HOME

Walking into Nikki's home in Charleston, South Carolina, you might think you've been transported into a glamorous black-and-white movie. Aside from a handful of bright green plants, the furnishings, paint, decor, and accessories are black and white, punctuated by dramatic silver chandeliers.

The entry leads right into a cozy family room, adorned with framed photos (black and white), a collection of her favorite books (black and white), and family albums and mementos stored in matching cloth binders (ivory!), all of which create a cohesive look on the shelves. Nikki organizes albums either by family member or by event, and her family loves to sit in the living room and flip through old photos together. She is the queen of creating special experiences for family members and guests—game nights, movie nights, s'mores stations—you name it, she's created it.

Since the home is without an entry closet or mudroom, a few flat trays slide out from under the couch, serving as a discreet drop station for guests to tuck away shoes by the front door.

Throughout her life, Nikki was often far away from loved ones, so now she loves to keep them close. The entire home is designed with entertaining in mind. The dining space is built for hosting intimate dinner parties, and Nikki uses dressers, china cabinets, and sideboards to corral and display her impressive assortment of serving bowls, platters, pitchers, candles, and barware. During our visit, she treats us to a perfect Southern meal composed of my very first shrimp and grits alongside glasses of sweet tea (served in mason jars, of course). Nikki shares that even when she orders takeout, she serves the food on beautiful platters with cloth napkins—presentation is everything!

In the kitchen, she repurposed a china cabinet she scored for $150 to create an inviting coffee and tea station. Mike was able to mount the top half of the cabinet to the wall to create a custom look, and the base was fashioned into storage in the dining room. Nikki loves making what's old new again.

The kitchen is comprised of carefully thought out "stations," including designated zones for beverage service, outdoor entertaining, everyday dining, baking, food prep, cleaning, and food storage. Under the kitchen sink, Nikki uses stackable containers filled with soap and cleaning supplies to conceal the unsightly pipes that are typically an eyesore in every home.

Since Mike and Nikki are now empty nesters, they turned a spare bedroom into a home theater for watching movies, which includes upholstered recliners, a platform for elevated seats, and a mini beverage fridge and snack station complete with individual treats, popcorn bowls, and cozy blankets. Let's just say my kids would never, ever leave. In the adjacent guest bedroom, Nikki has stocked the closet and bathroom with lavish amenities to ensure the comfort of her guests. She provides a supply of spare hangers, extra linens, and luxuries such as magazines, room spray, and a plush, white robe. In the guest bathroom she stocks a hair dryer, toothbrushes, bath salts, face oils, and scented candles. Please note that she does have a two-night-maximum policy since it would be natural for visitors to want to move in indefinitely.

Nikki's spacious home office serves as her base for creating content, recording videos, and meeting with virtual clients. There are no loose papers in sight, and instead of a filing cabinet, Nikki and her team use a labeled binder system. Her meticulously organized desk drawers prompt gasps.

Just down the road, her company is headquartered in a bright, sunny space with a kitchenette, stylish conference room (where workshops and organizing parties are held), and offices for each member of the team.

By adding a curtain and some shelves and decor, Nikki has transformed a slim utility closet in her home office into a quiet place for praying, drawing, writing, meditating, and Bible study. She loves to pin up prayers on the cloth board, and when they're answered she takes them down. Asked and answered. Art, books, journals, and mementos make the tiny space feel like a retreat.

This isn't the only closet in the home that has undergone a full makeover. Since Nikki and Mike rarely wear coats, she transformed their downstairs coat closet into a tiny pet paradise for her furry friends, Bentley and Albert. The walk-in closet is a joyful tribute to the two pups, complete with patterned wallpaper, painted portraits, cozy dog beds, and all the pet essentials, including toys, gear, brushes, treats, wipes for paws, and even their signature outfits.

Nikki loves to design her living spaces around her family's individual needs and values. Her garage (in addition to being functional storage space for tools and household supplies) serves double duty as a makeshift front porch. When the weather is nice, she loves to open the garage doors, set up chairs, and chitchat with the neighbors as they walk by. She designed the layout of the space so everything from gardening supplies to automotive care to barbecue gear is tucked away and stored in the wall-mounted storage system that lines each wall, leaving plenty of room for socializing, hobbies, projects, and relaxing. The lesson? Organize your home for how you want to live (and if at all possible, make yourself a home movie theater).

TIPS + TAKEAWAYS

- Create a comfort station for your guests. Nikki makes her guests feel welcome by stocking items such as throw blankets, spare umbrellas, cozy socks, to-go beverage tumblers, and even small gifts, like dark chocolate bars, for the road.

- Use a set of stackable containers to conceal the unsightly pipes beneath your bathroom and kitchen sink. Pull-out drawers create an easy-access storage solution.

- Banish the junk drawer, and say hello to the counter canister! Stock stylish canisters with high-access utility items. Pouches keep tiny items from getting lost in the shuffle.

- Use dressers or credenzas for stylish storage solutions in every room. Nikki paints her furniture and swaps hardware, so each piece feels cohesive within the rest of her home.

- Get the look: Try using a single-color palette like Nikki to create a unified aesthetic. Nikki remembers her mother always had one all-white room in the home, which felt like heaven.

- Want to access something from deep storage without searching through every bin in sight? Nikki uses the ToteScan app to inventory the contents of each bin in her garage. She can pull up the contents of each bin in a flash just by scanning the QR code. Brilliant!

Q/A WITH NIKKI BOYD

FAVORITE SPACE TO ORGANIZE?
My favorite space to organize is a drawer! I love organizing desk drawers and kitchen drawers. There is something that makes me want to sing every time I open a beautifully organized drawer.

DIRTY LITTLE CLUTTER SECRET?
The bench in front of my bed is my dirty little secret. It is my go-to place to put everything as I enter my room, and it's often a clutter zone.

MOST TREASURED POSSESSION?
My most treasured possession is my teacup lamp. It is actually a lamp I made, but what makes it so special is it was the first project I ever shared on YouTube and was the start of my career as a professional organizer.

GREATEST EXTRAVAGANCE?
Our lawn robot that maintains our lawn.

FAVORITE ORGANIZING TIP OR IDEA?
Creating a home-management center. A place where you can easily grab those essentials such as a tape measure, flashlight, and scissors and easily put them back. Basically, anything that you are always looking to grab.

WHAT DO YOU DO WHEN YOU FEEL OVERWHELMED IN A HOME OR SPACE?
Divide the space into four sections, and start with one section at a time.

MOST COMMON MISCONCEPTION ABOUT PRO ORGANIZERS?
That pro organizers only work with stuff. As a pro organizer, many of my clients work with me to help them with productivity and creating systems to help improve their home and work life.

BEST ADVICE FOR ASPIRING ENTREPRENEURS?
Planning without action is actually fear in disguise. You simply need to start.

BIGGEST TAKEAWAY OR LESSON LEARNED FROM ORGANIZING OTHER PEOPLE'S HOMES?
You have to meet people where they are in order to move them toward having a well-organized home.

ACTUAL MORNING ROUTINE?
After my shower and getting dressed, I start my day with a cup of coffee, devotional time, and then map out my day in my planner.

ACTUAL EVENING ROUTINE?
After dinner and my evening shower, I usually spend the evening relaxing with my husband and pups, then read five chapters in my Bible before going to bed.

ONE SELF-CARE TIP YOU FOLLOW?
I have things that I do for my daily self-care that just start my day beautifully. One is my gratitude journal. Starting my day by writing down the things that I am grateful for always gives me a boost.

THE MOST VALUABLE CAREER ADVICE YOU'VE EVER BEEN GIVEN?
Everyone has advice but listen to those who have done it for themselves.

FAVORITE GIFT TO GIVE?
Tiffany wineglasses. My friend had a tradition of sending me Tiffany wineglasses for my birthday, and getting that blue box was always so exciting. So I started giving them as a gift also.

WHAT MIGHT PEOPLE BE SURPRISED TO LEARN ABOUT YOU?
That I have never eaten rice before. My mom cooked it just about every day, but even as a baby I would never eat it. I just recently had sushi for the first time, and they had to make it without the rice.

GO-TO DAILY UNIFORM?
Jeans and a tee with my black Converse.

ASHLEY MURPHY

THE TRADITIONAL-WITH-A-TWIST FARMHOUSE

ASHLEY'S STORY

How does a fitness instructor from a small town in Ohio become the cofounder of the largest home-organizing franchise in the world? It turns out that following your passion and investing in relationships can go a long way.

Ashley caught the organizing bug early but never dreamt it could become a full-time and successful career. As an only child, clutter made her anxious, and she spent a lot of time tidying and rearranging her room. In college she developed a reputation for folding and organizing her friends' clothes and keeping her own space meticulously organized. After receiving a degree in fashion merchandising from Indiana University, Ashley moved to Chicago for her first job as a buyer at a boutique. She quickly realized she was more interested in wellness than in fashion and returned to school for a certification in health and fitness. After completing her program, she worked for a luxury in-home personal training company, and when business slowed due to the recession, Ashley offered to help organize her clients' kitchens to optimize their health. Luckily, many of them were game, and soon after, she and a friend launched Neat Chicago, a small organizing business. They created a website and had just started seeing clients when Ashley's husband was relocated to California for a new job opportunity.

A chance encounter with a total stranger in San Francisco would change everything. Ashley had popped into a boutique while exploring her new city and met Molly Graves, another Chicago transplant who had also just moved to San Francisco for a similar reason. They chatted it up for a few minutes and had so much in common they decided to meet for coffee the next day (as the story goes, Molly actually chased Ashley down the street to grab her number). Over coffee, they discovered that they also had a shared love for organizing. Molly had recently started taking closet-organizing clients through the boutique, and although dormant since her move, Ashley still had her Neat Chicago brand. By the end of the coffee date, the two had sufficiently bonded and decided to launch a new organizing brand together called Neat San Francisco. Ashley recalls that they liked and trusted each other instantly, so starting a business with a perfect stranger didn't seem as crazy as it sounds.

The duo started working with their first clients in the San Francisco Bay Area, and when they expanded into other nearby cities, they decided to rebrand from Neat San Francisco to Neat Method—inspired by Ashley's background in the fitness industry, where the term *method* is commonly used. It didn't take long for their business to flourish through word of mouth and referrals. Clients loved their signature stylish aesthetic and full-service approach that included move management, unpacking, and luxury organizing for every room in the home. The dynamic duo realized they could successfully design spaces and implement organizing systems without involving their clients at all—a huge win for the busy demographic they served who craved neat and stylish spaces but weren't able to participate in the process.

When Ashley's husband was offered a new job, which required relocating back to Chicago, she and Molly seized the opportunity to try growing their brand in a new city. They hired a mutual friend, Marissa Hagmeyer (who became one of their first official employees and is now a full-time partner), to help launch the brand in the Chicago area. Only eight months later, Marissa's husband was transferred to a new job in Fort Lauderdale, Florida, and they took the leap to start a third operation in Florida (notice a theme here?). Now, with three successful markets launched, they received inquiries from others who were interested in learning from Neat Method to establish their own organizing businesses in other cities. This resulted in a key decision: to start licensing their brand to others so they could expand across the United States. Using the well-established Neat Method techniques, logo, and brand, new organizers gained the confidence to take their own leaps into the world of entrepreneurship.

Soon after, Whitmor, a product manufacturing company, offered to acquire the company, which helped them scale even further. They were then able to design and launch their first product line. Another leap!

Once acquired, Ashley and her cofounders moved from licensing other organizers to a more formalized franchising process. This move proved to be wildly successful for growth and a win for new organizers seeking support and community (they now have ninety-five franchise owners across the United States and Canada). Franchise owners undergo a rigorous application process to gain access to training, mentorship, resources, support, a referral program, and a community of other female entrepreneurs to launch and grow their own businesses.

As the business expanded, Ashley and her partners, Molly and Marissa, transitioned from hands-on organizing to business growth and operations.

Ashley handles franchise operations, and Marissa oversees the development and growth of their curated product line, which you can find at Bloomingdale's, Anthropologie, and at www.neatmethod.com. Molly is still onboard as a silent partner and keeps things neat in Hawaiʻi with her family.

Neat Method is currently the largest organizing franchise in the world, and they receive thousands of applications a year from organizers who want to join the company. Ashley attributes the success of the business to a combination of grit, hard work, and strong relationship-building. "We never expected this and never even knew we were capable of it. At the end of the day, we just love what we do, and it's all about friendship and connection. That's what makes the world go around, right?"

ASHLEY'S HOME

Built in 1873, Ashley's home, which she shares with her husband and two boys, is situated on a picturesque block in a Chicago suburb. The house is full of original character, details, and charm, but short on storage, so Ashley teamed up with designer Kate Marker to install hardworking (but stylish!) systems throughout the home. In the mudroom, a slim custom cabinet was installed to house coats, seasonal accessories, and running shoes, which are tossed discreetly into woven baskets. Next to the cabinet, a wooden bench provides a place to tuck winter boots, and stylish brass hooks create additional storage for hanging coats and bags. Here's proof that a functional entry can be composed from nothing more than a single rod, a few hooks, and a handful of shelves.

In her boys' rooms, small closets are used to store their favorite books, games, toys, and even LEGOs at arm's reach for quick access and independent clean up. She's even reserved a few spare shelves to display their most

treasured LEGO creations. Pro tip: Ashley has set up a "transition bin" for broken or incomplete LEGO projects her boys want to work on. When it comes to room decor for her kids, removeable star decals create the look of custom wallpaper without the commitment or the price tag. Throughout the rest of the home, she uses existing furniture, such as credenzas and built-in cabinets, to tuck away games, art supplies, and toys.

With no linen closet to speak of, Ashley's family owns just one set of sheets per bed. Sheets are washed and immediately returned to each bed—no storage (or folding) necessary! This genius space-saving hack might just come home with me.

In the laundry room, Ashley has created a practical and stylish storage setup using the Neat Method product line: metal bins with magnetic labels corral cleaning products, sun and bug sprays, and pet supplies, while a turntable displays detergent and wool dryer balls in a sleek glass canister, elevating the utilitarian objects in the home to make the household chores a little more pleasant.

An expansive island with barstools in the kitchen serves as the family gathering place for snacking, homework, and socializing. There's plenty of built-in storage to conceal pots and pans, food storage, baking supplies, and kitchen gadgets, while open shelves display everyday plates and bowls, pretty vases, and ceramics. To create a stylish food pantry, she's dedicated a set of shelves for nonperishable items, corralling food staples into open baskets and labeled glass jars with wooden lids. Just below, a wide drawer is a grab-and-go kid snack station stocked with individual bars, chips, and crackers. Expandable wooden drawer organizers are inserted to create a custom look and help maintain order. Frequent-use spices have been decanted into labeled jars, and Ashley has added a "backup spices bin" just above (genius move alert!), so she can refill and replenish spices when necessary.

Ashley's home office is a sunny and inviting space with a view on to the yard. Given her hectic schedule, she keeps her workspace especially minimal and serene. Her wooden desk contains only her computer, a lamp, and a few decorative objects, while a wall-mounted shelving unit displays plants, art books, and framed photos, as well as her minimal office supplies arranged neatly on a white tray.

Ashley's entire home feels luxurious, intentional, and elevated. Her cozy living spaces consist of velvet upholstered seating and pillows in rich jewel tones, and her formal dining room is punctuated by a dramatic chandelier, patterned wallpaper, and heavy drapes. While the home has a more formal feel than some, it's still warm and inviting, like Ashley herself. During our visit, Ashley's boys bound in from school and snuggle with their puppy before grabbing snacks and curling up to play games together at the coffee table. Family living at its best!

Ashley has managed to create the seemingly impossible—an easy-to-maintain, stylish, organized, and comfortable family home.

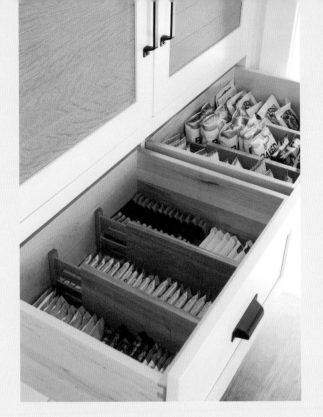

TIPS + TAKEAWAYS

· Pick a color scheme for utilitarian objects (wine openers, can openers, salad servers, utensils) which will level up your kitchen drawers and create a cohesive look.

· Decanting trick! Set up a "backup bin" for bulk pantry staples that don't fit into your existing jars so you can refill and replenish instead of wasting the excess.

· Small-space hack: Use a single set of high-quality sheets for each bed so you never have to fold or store your linens. Ditto for bath towels. Use, wash, and use again.

· Set up a "transition bin" for broken or incomplete LEGO projects. No more tripping over LEGO parts. Ouch!

· Store office and household supplies in matching labeled bins tucked neatly out of sight to keep your work surface clean and clear.

· No entry closet? No problem. Ashley added a custom built-in cabinet with a rod and shelves to her entry, but you can also purchase a freestanding unit or simply add hooks and a bench with cubbies (for shoes) below.

Q/A WITH ASHLEY MURPHY

WHAT DO YOU LOVE MOST ABOUT YOUR HOME?
That it's old! We bought it knowing we were going to need to rehab it, and little by little we have. Each new space brings me so much happiness, just knowing all the love that has been put into changing it.

FAVORITE SPACE TO ORGANIZE?
Kitchen.

DIRTY LITTLE CLUTTER SECRET?
Depends on the month, but I'd probably have to say our basement.

CAN'T-LIVE-WITHOUT ORGANIZING PRODUCT?
Neat Method's acacia drawer dividers.

WHAT'S IN YOUR ORGANIZING TOOLKIT?
In my organizing days, I felt a little like Mary Poppins with the amount of stuff that I would magically store all in one bag. You could find anything from labels to box cutters, Band-Aids to granola bars.

FAVORITE ORGANIZING HACK?
Museum gel to stop a product from sliding in a drawer.

WHAT DO YOU DO WHEN YOU FEEL OVERWHELMED IN A HOME OR SPACE?
Start with the smallest space, like a drawer, and build out from there.

MOST COMMON MISCONCEPTION ABOUT PRO ORGANIZERS?
That our homes are always perfect. Life still happens for us as well!

ACTUAL MORNING ROUTINE?
5 a.m. wake up. Lemon water, coffee, catch up on emails and work projects in complete silence until 7. Get kids fed and out the door. 9 a.m. yoga and then my workday of calls begins!

ACTUAL EVENING ROUTINE?
4 p.m. finish working. Open wine, start dinner, and listen to music. Hang with kids, 9 p.m. bedtime for kids. Enjoy the calm with a show that I barely make it through. Asleep by 10.

ONE SELF-CARE TIP YOU FOLLOW?
This is something that I've tried hard to achieve. For so long, I put work and my kids in front of everything else (mostly taking care of me), and it began to catch up to me. Changing my schedule to early mornings of work so that I could justify my 9 a.m. "me time" made a huge difference.

BIGGEST PERSONAL HOME-ORGANIZING CHALLENGE?
Our basement. It's the space that's out of sight and out of mind. It then just accumulates all of the "junk" until I can't take it anymore.

THE MOST VALUABLE CAREER ADVICE YOU'VE EVER BEEN GIVEN?
Lean on your people! Building with a team of hardworking women has been the most valuable decision I've ever made. And it's fun at the same time! A win-win when it comes to working!

HOW DO YOU RECHARGE WHEN IT'S ALL TOO MUCH?
I practice yoga regularly (four to five times per week). It gives me the mental pause and daily reset to allow me to approach the day with my best intentions.

FAVORITE GIFT TO GIVE?
Any type of facial serum or cute pajama set! I find that neither are items we typically buy for ourselves yet are so fun to receive!

A CURATED STUDIO
IN BROOKLYN

LAURA'S STORY

Laura Cattano has always lived by her own rules. Raised on Long Island, New York, and the youngest of five kids, Laura clearly remembers pushing her sister's stuff to her side of their shared room to keep her own space pristine. Early on, she set herself apart from her friends by listening to different music, dressing in her own style (opting to wear heels and dress clothes to school when everyone else was in jeans and sneakers), and dismissing trends in favor of what felt authentic to her.

After studying environmental science in college, Laura moved to New York City to pursue acting. She needed a job to keep her financially afloat while auditioning for roles and landed a job with the legendary interior designer Vicente Wolf. Working with Wolf opened Laura's eyes to an entirely new world and sparked her love of aesthetics and design.

Laura's transition to organization started when she organized Wolf's design studio. She overhauled and optimized every square inch of the resource room—meticulously organizing and alphabetizing everything, including the client files, binders, and resource books.

Once she'd whipped the design studio into shape, she turned her attention toward her own apartment. A self-described former shopaholic, Laura looked around her home and realized that she was surrounded by many items that she'd wanted in the moment but didn't actually love. She challenged herself to take a one-month shopping break and reclaimed the time she would have spent shopping (and returning things) to thoughtfully reconsider her lifestyle. She asked herself these pointed questions:

How do I want my home to look, feel, and function?

How do I want to dress and present myself?

How do I want to design and set up my space?

When she had clear answers, Laura embarked on a deliberate quest to evaluate each item she owned and determine if it was adding or subtracting value from her life. She transformed her relationship with her possessions and started investing in the *right things* instead of *all of the things*. Laura's experience not only changed how she felt about her space and stuff but improved and enriched every aspect of her life.

It was through the process of re-creating her own home and spending countless hours studying storage solutions that Laura realized her interest in organization had surpassed her interest in theater. She officially decided to make a career shift. Soon after, she was approached by a top marketing executive who was looking for some help organizing her life. Laura seized the opportunity to announce that she was offering home-organizing services, made up a rate on the spot, and landed her first paid organizing job. She created a website and branded herself as a professional organizer and interior stylist. It was 2005—long before home organizing had become a national phenomenon.

Laura's clean, elevated aesthetic and sharp eye for design set her apart, and her business grew quickly through word of mouth. Based in New York, where square footage is often limited, Laura has dedicated her lengthy career to helping people live the lives that they want on their own terms and within the space that they have.

As Laura's work garnered press mentions and her reputation grew, she made the decision not to scale or grow a team. Instead she remains committed to serving a small roster of hand-selected clients, including many with whom she's been working for years. "My work is very personal. As a self-reformed shopaholic, I live what I am teaching my clients. This is more than a fad diet, it's a lifestyle shift that I know can change a life because it changed mine." Nearly two decades into a thriving career, Laura's mission remains the same: to help her clients change their relationship with their stuff and elevate their homes and lives.

LAURA'S HOME

The first thing that strikes me when I walk into Laura's 335-square-foot Brooklyn apartment is that every single inch feels considered. It feels like a jewel box filled with treasures, and looking around at the bright, open space, it's evident that each item she owns has been thoughtfully and carefully curated. The fact that her home is a rental has done nothing to deter Laura from customizing every detail to her exact style and specifications. She personally spray painted the radiator off-white, hand-painted the wood floors the perfect shade of greige ("Drop Cloth" by Farrow & Ball, for inquiring minds), and even tied a wall of fake ivy to the fire escape to create a privacy shield, blocking her view of the neighboring apartments. To break up the small studio space into clear zones, she ordered custom wooden room dividers with mirror accents. In the bathroom, she eliminated the medicine cabinet, swapped light fixtures, and added wall shelves and storage cabinets to store her toiletries. The floating shelves in the bathroom were cut to size, caulked, and secured with brackets. All cords and light switches have been corralled and concealed using Command cord clips and Velcro.

Even her furniture was specifically handmade for the space—she designed a small limestone dining table with a plywood cylinder base, at which we ate lunch during my visit (I was very, very careful not to spill my food!), and commissioned a custom bed to fit her space. The bed was constructed using a headboard, wooden base, and a custom-size mattress (smaller than a twin), which her friends lovingly refer to as "the crib." Her bed faces the perfectly styled closet, which Laura personally constructed out of shelves from IKEA. For Christmas, she even asked her mom for a pipe cutter to custom cut rods for her closet and for client projects. Little details, big impact.

This one-room home is a study in brilliant small-space solutions. Instead of bulky bathroom accessories, Laura opts for a travel-size iron, steamer, and hair dryer, which fit in a single bin in her bathroom. She trimmed a canvas shoe organizer in half vertically to fit her tiny coat closet. Instead of a full-size television, Laura's computer serves double duty as her TV when needed. Towels are neatly folded on the bathroom shelves, and Laura owns only a single set of high-quality sheets she washes and dries the same day so she can happily live without a linen closet. Archival items such as tax docs and sentimental photos are tucked away above the fridge in stackable white boxes, and lingerie, pj's, workout clothes, and extra hangers are neatly stored in canvas boxes under the bed. She contains client notebooks, magazines, and current papers in sleek, brown boxes and uses larger white closet boxes to store household essentials, like paper goods.

While Laura does own a full wardrobe and impressive shoe and handbag collection, she doesn't like to be distracted by clothes that are off-season, so she carefully stows out-of-season items in chic storage boxes. She uses her seasonal wardrobe swaps as an opportunity to clean out both her closet and clothes and to reacquaint herself with what she owns, reevaluate her style, and set up a wardrobe that not only suits the current season but also her taste and lifestyle.

Laura opts to invest in the highest quality for many of the things she brings into her space, splurging on custom furniture, art, and decor by Vitsœ, Kristina Dam Studio, Ilka Kramer, Nancy Kwon, and others. But when it comes to storage solutions and accessories, she sources from retail chains such as IKEA, MUJI, and CB2. The mix of styles achieves the perfect aesthetic balance she's after.

Laura's home has a clear point of view and reflects her style, values, and preferences. Her home, life, and philosophy serve as a reminder to all of us to look around and question what we own and how we set up our own spaces. While her style is decidedly modern and minimal, Laura bristles when I refer to her as a minimalist (she doesn't like rules or labels and proudly owns twenty-six handbags). When I offer that my definition of minimalism is more rooted in intentionality than a prescribed way of living or specific quantity of items, she nods and summarizes her philosophy in a single sentence. "Know who you are and how you want to live, and look at everything as a tool." It's clear that Laura has done just that.

TIPS + TAKEAWAYS

· Question the rules and customize your space to fit your unique needs.

· Think outside of the box and shop different departments for your home accessories (Laura uses a small rug as her bathmat, a real curtain instead of a traditional shower curtain, and even a cheeseboard to elevate her bathroom candles and accessories).

· Organize by how you use things. We've all heard the advice "group like things together," but it's also important to group things together based on how you use them. For instance, T-shirts fall into multiple categories that do not belong together: workout, sleep, nice ones you wear out, and ones you keep only for the memories.

· Balance your use of open and closed storage. Maximize existing closets (closed storage) for utility items you don't want or need to look at, so you can use the open storage to display the things you care about, like a favorite painting or a beloved vase.

· No need to break the bank to have fine art in your home. Frame art pics from design books in simple frames for an elevated look that's easy on the wallet.

· Tuck personal memorabilia that you may not want to publicly display in clever hidden spots around your home.

Q/A WITH LAURA CATTANO

WHAT DO YOU LOVE MOST ABOUT YOUR HOME?
I love that everywhere I look I see only things I cherish.

BIGGEST HOME-ORGANIZING CHALLENGE?
Fitting everything I own in a 335-square-foot studio, while still feeling spacious and not looking like a storage unit.

WHAT ARE YOU THE PROUDEST OF?
Building my business with no connections, no money, no PR or marketing strategy. My success is a direct result of following my intuition and trusting my talent.

FAVORITE SPACE TO ORGANIZE?
The closet.

DIRTY LITTLE CLUTTER SECRET?
Nope.

WHAT IS YOUR GREATEST EXTRAVAGANCE?
I am a Taurus—my whole life is an extravagance. Clothes, furniture, home accessories, living in NYC, travel, dinners, taxis . . .

FAVORITE ORGANIZING HACK?
Invest in beautiful glass candles so you can repurpose the vessels for storing makeup brushes, lip glosses, and small tools in the bathroom.

YOUR DEFINITION OF ORGANIZATION?
People conflate being organized with being neat and/or clean, but these are three different things. Being organized is simply knowing what you have and where to find it. For me, an organized space is one where the experience of doing something is intuitive, graceful, and enjoyable.

WHAT DO YOU DO WHEN YOU FEEL OVERWHELMED IN A HOME OR SPACE?
I remind myself I am the one in control, that things can overwhelm you only if you give them the power to do so. Then I get to it.

BIGGEST TAKEAWAY OR LESSON LEARNED FROM ORGANIZING OTHER PEOPLE'S HOMES?
Everyone has different preferences. One person may be bothered by something, and the next person won't even notice. It's the reason a one-size-fits-all approach never works.

BEST ADVICE FOR ASPIRING ENTREPRENEURS?
Do the work. There are no shortcuts. The only way to have longevity is to actually provide people with an amazing service every time.

WHAT MIGHT PEOPLE BE SURPRISED TO LEARN ABOUT YOU?
I think people are surprised that I'm not type A, that I'm not as disciplined and regimented as I might look.

ACTUAL MORNING ROUTINE?
I'm most productive in the morning. I make my bed, do a light workout, check emails and social media, and have a light breakfast. Morning is the time to clean up my space so that at the end of the day I'm coming home to serenity.

ACTUAL EVENING ROUTINE?
Years ago, I decided whenever possible to take evenings off, which means no client calls or emails. When not out with friends I am home enjoying a meal and a movie. I shower to transition from day to evening, and I have a strict lighting schedule (limiting light sources by the hour to coordinate with the sun) so I'm totally relaxed and in bed by 10 p.m. at the latest.

DAILY UNIFORM?
I don't own sneakers, shorts, or anything uber casual. My go-to is something modern, chic, and elegant.

Disclaimer: The intention of this book is not to encourage you to buy more *stuff* to put your *stuff* in, tempting as it may be. During the process of interviewing the twenty-five organizers featured here, I was struck by how many of them mentioned their longing to live with (and manage) less stuff. A simple truth: The less we own, the less we have to clean, organize, store, manage, and eventually dispose of. The good news is that one of the most sustainable practices we can implement is simply to buy less and use the things we already own. Better for our wallets and the planet, so count me IN. Of course, one of the inevitable parts of the home-organizing process is investing in containment and storage solutions for the things you do need, use, and love, so here are a few easy ways to lighten your environmental footprint as you get organized.

GET CREATIVE WITH STORAGE
Instead of buying new organizing products, repurpose what you've got. Mason jars, shoe boxes, makeup pouches, pencil cases, and toolboxes all make great storage vessels and are probably hiding out somewhere in your home already.

INVEST IN NATURAL MATERIALS
I probably don't have to tell you how bad plastic is for the environment, but in a nutshell, it never breaks down, pollutes our oceans, clogs our land-fills, and makes the fish and dolphins super sad. Luckily there are plenty of stylish and functional alternatives to plastic containers, like wood, glass, metal, cotton, rattan, and other natural materials, which are easy on the eyes and better for the planet.

TRY THE "RULE OF ONE"
Opt for quality instead of quantity when investing in frequent-use items like sunglasses, umbrellas, wallets, and water bottles. Owning "less but better" means you're more likely to care for the things you own and less likely to lose or misplace them.

OPT FOR REUSABLE INSTEAD OF DISPOSABLE
Shopping bags, water bottles, plastic straws, sandwich bags, paper towels, cotton rounds, your kitchen sponge—you name it, there's now a reus-able, plastic-free version. Do your best to stop buying disposable items and swap in reusable alternatives.

REPAIR BEFORE YOU REPLACE
Do your research and invest in products that are known for their quality and will stand the test of time. When something you own does break, check to see if you can sew, mend, or fix it before toss-ing. Many companies will stand by their products and offer free repairs for life. For items such as electronics that are beyond repair, seek out your local e-waste drop-off center.

SHOP THE BULK BINS

Product packaging is a massive source of waste in our landfills. Shopping the bulk bins and bringing your own cloth bags or glass containers can make a huge impact when it comes to reducing single-use plastics. Many refill shops now offer a range of package-free bath, body, cooking, kitchen, and cleaning products in refillable containers. BYOB (bring your own bag) and start refilling!

SHOP SMALL AND LOCAL

Vote with your wallet and support small brands and independent retailers. Buying locally not only supports your local community and economy, but also reduces shipping and packaging waste so you can reduce your carbon footprint.

DONATE RESPONSIBLY

Repeat after me: clothing is not trash! If you find yourself in an "everything must go" mode, make a donation plan for the items you want to part with.

Charity shops, churches, schools, nonprofits, parent groups, community centers, and local buy-nothing groups are all great options for items that are in good condition. Also, take advantage of local creative reuse centers, textile recycling centers, and e-waste drop-off locations for the items that can't be donated.

TRY A PURCHASE PAUSE

A great way to become more intentional with how you consume is to curb spending all together for a set period of time. If you're drowning in clutter, struggling with consumer debt, or just tired of facing buyer's remorse, a spending freeze might be just what the doctor ordered. Curbing your spending on nonessential items (even for a few weeks) can help you shift your perspective and spending habits, become a more mindful consumer, and inspire you to find healthier alternatives to recreational shopping.

THE ZERO WASTE HOME

JULIEN'S STORY

Julien grew up in a tiny hilltop town in Langres, France, in a small, modest apartment. Raised by parents who placed little emphasis on material things, he learned early to value community and connection over consumption. Small town living made for an easy, happy life. Julien studied dance, art, drama, and music, and had an active social life going to parties and enjoying dinners and social gatherings with family and friends.

Curious about the world outside of his small town, Julien left for university at eighteen, and after receiving multiple degrees (business studies, applied languages, and a master's degree in marketing), he moved to Dublin with his boyfriend, who was pursuing a law degree. Eager to see the world, the couple lived, studied, and worked in Brussels, Montreal, and Luxembourg before making a more permanent home in Paris, where they purchased their first home.

It was a confluence of factors that would spark Julien's passion for decluttering, organization, and environmentalism. Losing his stepmother (with whom he was very close) was a catalyst to help his father (who was physically and mentally disabled at the time) clean out his entire home and simplify his life. Julien underwent a long and detailed process to help his father evaluate and edit all his belongings. He learned how to successfully coach him through the difficult process and researched how and where to donate responsibly. Around the same time, he started reading about sustainability and the zero-waste movement. He watched movies and documentaries and devoured books on the subject, including *Zero Waste Home* by Bea Johnson and *L'art de la Simplicité* by Dominique Loreau, which greatly inspired him. He and his partner, Gregory (who is also passionate about sustainability), decided to go all in on zero-waste living in their newly purchased home. The first step? Curbing spending (no new things) in an effort to resist the "curse of consumerism." Rather than feeling restrictive, not buying anything felt liberating to Julien. Resisting the constant societal pressure to consume was empowering, and he felt like he was making a political statement with his new lifestyle. He focused on using up the products he already owned (no more cabinets full of half-used products) and simultaneously started letting go of things he didn't need, use, or love. It took over a year to fully process all his belongings and find new homes for the items he wanted to let go of. The result was not only an organized, clutter-free home, but a life that felt more authentic and meaningful.

In 2017 Julien discovered home organizing as a profession. He was thrilled at the opportunity to share what he had learned about zero-waste living and searched the internet to locate local organizers. He found Elodie Wery, who had already established a successful organizing business (Elodie, Thibaut & Co) and offered courses for new organizers in France. Julien trained with Elodie, whose philosophy was well-matched with his own, launched a website, and started taking clients right away—primarily direct referrals from Elodie. Julien is one of the few professional organizers in this book who chose to keep his day job while also launching a business. The reason? He genuinely enjoyed both careers. He has worked as an actor on the stage, done human-centered work with a nonprofit that helps the elderly, and is currently working as an event planner for a company that leads philanthropic-based team-building events throughout Paris. Despite his full-time job, he's managing to take on home-organizing clients and has developed his own unique process and methodology rooted in his passion for eco-friendly living.

Ironically, his work as a home organizer is less focused on organization (although he admits it's a positive byproduct of his work) and more driven by intentionality. He begins each project with a coffee date to meet and understand his clients before helping them move out items that don't align with their vision and values. What sets his method apart is his total commitment to sustainability and zero-waste living. In addition to composting, recycling, and upcycling, he insists on finding new homes for every single item that his clients no longer want, thereby avoiding having anything go to the landfill. His passion for environmentalism and sustainability anchors his daily life and is integral to his work with clients. His brand of environmentalism is rooted in optimism and a deep desire to do better and treat our planet with care. "I just love giving things a second life."

JULIEN'S HOME

Julien's house tour begins with chocolate croissants and ends with a tutorial on how to make zero-waste deodorant. The flat that he owns with Gregory (his partner of twenty-two years) resides in a historic building in the Belleville neighborhood of Paris on the same block Édith Piaf (one of France's most legendary singers) lived. While the building itself is full of charm and original historic details, it came with more than a few challenges. When they purchased the flat, it was run down and had an awkward, outdated floor plan, so Julien redesigned the layout (he and his father-in-law did the plumbing and moved the toilet!), installed windows between rooms to create more light, painted the entire place, and added bright, patterned wallpaper. Just prior to my visit, an old pipe burst in his upstairs neighbor's flat, which resulted in flooding and subsequent patching, painting, and repairs. Despite the occasional challenge, Julien loves his home and has enjoyed making it comfortable, inviting, and brimming with personality.

Instead of splurging on new furniture and decor, nearly every item in the flat has been creatively sourced secondhand: furniture passed down by family, picked up from thrift stores, or even discovered on the street and lovingly rehabbed. In the cheerful living room, new cushion inserts have revived a corduroy couch his parents bought in 1974. Armchairs are accented with pillows his mother embroidered decades ago, and functional decor, including an oversize vase and charming vintage fan, were treasures from the sidewalk. Each item in the home has a history.

When it comes to decor, Julien is especially resourceful. The simple pair of glass bottles that function as pretty candlestick holders used to contain his father's medication. He's framed everything from old T-shirts to postcards, creating new art from old and inherited objects. In the hallway, four tiny magazine clippings are displayed in matching gold frames he scored for a single Euro. I also learn that all his Christmas decor was found on the street or even in the garbage. A huge Madonna fan, Julien was overjoyed to stumble upon a stack of vintage Madonna records, which are propped up and displayed as treasures in his living room. He tells me these happy accidents happen all the time when you are open to them. "People have far too much and often leave it behind."

In the dining room, old cabinets and wall shelving have been refinished and painted. Another street find? The pendant light. While Julien typically donates his books after reading them (I was treated to one on my visit), he displays his favorites throughout the home on simple wall-mounted shelves. In keeping with his zero-waste lifestyle, Julien opts for long-lasting plants and dried florals to decorate his living spaces.

Since Julien and Gregory are roughly the same size, they share clothes and shoes (the majority once belonged to Julien's father), all of which fit on a single wardrobe rack and in a tiny dresser. An oversize, sturdy paper bag serves as their dual laundry bag, and to maximize hanging storage, repurposed soda can tabs are looped over individual hangers, adding a clever hook for another hanger—double the fun and zero waste!

In the tiny bathroom, Julien and Gregory own only five products between them (yes, that's right, FIVE): soap, lotion, toothpaste, grooming tonic for hair, and homemade zero-waste deodorant. The deodorant is made from a concoction of coconut oil, baking soda, cornstarch, and essential oil (I asked for a demo!), which he keeps in a small mason jar and says works like a charm.

It's easy to stay organized when you own only the essentials. A single box tucked under the bed contains old letters, photos, and passports, while a small cabinet in the dining room houses all of the couple's paperwork. Julien explains that most items are digitized, and all his personal and professional papers fit into one compact binder. Instead of the typical overstuffed medicine cabinet, Julien reveals a compact first-aid box stocked with a few medicines and essential oils.

Having a small space doesn't deter Julien from hosting and entertaining. He loves to throw dinner parties and can squeeze twelve people around the table, or more if standing or gathered in their cozy living room. Music is always playing (Gregory plays the piano), friends frequently pop over for a meal or a drink, and neighbors have become dear friends. Julien has created an intentional home that reflects who he is and what he cares about most: "I don't care about objects, I know all my neighbors, and it's like a family here."

TIPS + TAKEAWAYS

· Get resourceful and creative when it comes to furnishing your home. Check your local secondhand shops, buy-nothing community groups, flea markets, and estate sales to find treasures (often for a steal!).

· Create your own zero-waste art: frame a T-shirt, magazine cutout, or old postcard.

· Clean and reuse glass wine or milk bottles as zero-waste vases or candlestick holders.

· Hook a tab from a soda can over a clothes hanger to create another hook to hang an additional hanger, and maximize space in your closet. Remember Julien's mantra: "Zero waste and zero dollars!"

· Make your own zero-waste products. Baking soda and vinegar can be used to create cleaning products, stain remover, and even natural deodorant.

· Short on dresser space? Tuck pj's under your pillows for easy access before bed.

· Try a purchase pause. Taking a break from buying new things will help save you money, reduce clutter in your home, and positively impact the planet.

Q/A WITH JULIEN FEBVRE

BIGGEST HOME-ORGANIZING CHALLENGE?
My bedroom because it's a small room and I needed to create a space for sleeping and a space for storing my clothes. It has changed many times! And still more changes are on the way!

WHAT ARE YOU MOST PROUD OF?
My wardrobe that reflects who I am today. I can create much more now than before when I had many clothes that didn't reflect my style.

FAVORITE SPACE TO ORGANIZE?
Wardrobes and papers.

DIRTY LITTLE CLUTTER SECRET?
Under my bed, I could do much better (like having nothing).

MOST TREASURED POSSESSION?
An armchair that I really love, where I sit and watch movies or read a book.

GREATEST EXTRAVAGANCE?
Having many dresses that clients have given me during decluttering sessions. I keep them for crazy parties with friends!

WHAT'S IN YOUR ORGANIZING TOOLKIT?
The first and most important step: Decluttering. Ask yourself, "Do I use it? Do I like it?" The second step is to always wait before buying anything. No other tools.

FAVORITE ORGANIZING TIP OR IDEA?
Organizing by color (for clothes), organizing by dates (for papers), organizing by categories (for kitchen).

WHAT DO YOU DO WHEN YOU FEEL OVERWHELMED IN A HOME OR SPACE?
I go out, walk, breathe, and get refreshed. Usually when you don't think, ideas and solutions pop up immediately.

MOST COMMON MISCONCEPTION ABOUT PRO ORGANIZERS?
They do exactly what you could do on your own.

YOUR DEFINITION OF ORGANIZED?
A space in which each object has its own place.

BIGGEST TAKEAWAY OR LESSON LEARNED FROM ORGANIZING OTHER PEOPLE'S HOMES?
Each person is different, each mission is different.

ACTUAL MORNING ROUTINE?
Wake up; drink two glasses of water; eat a banana; do a quick cleaning (kitchen and bedroom); do a thirty-minute sport/yoga class; shower; eat eggs, coffee, and cereal; feed the chicken in the garden; meditate for ten minutes.

ACTUAL EVENING ROUTINE?
Switch off phone, computer, TV; drink a glass of water; brush teeth; read a book for fifteen to thirty minutes; sleep.

THE MOST VALUABLE CAREER ADVICE YOU'VE EVER BEEN GIVEN?
You will usually have a positive response if you ask for and say what you want.

HOW DO YOU RECHARGE WHEN IT'S ALL TOO MUCH?
Walk a lot with music. I avoid the phone, social media, and any Wi-Fi!

FAVORITE GIFT TO GIVE?
A bottle of wine.

WHAT MIGHT PEOPLE BE SURPRISED TO LEARN ABOUT YOU?
I was a dancer and an actor once in my life.

GO-TO DAILY UNIFORM?
A pair of jeans, a white T-shirt, and a cool sweatshirt.

JEAN GORDON

A CREATIVE COUPLE'S CITY ESCAPE

JEAN'S STORY

The youngest of four siblings and the daughter of a police officer, Jean was raised in Queens, New York, in a tiny row house filled with a lot of people and a lot of action. While the rest of the family was unfazed by the often disorderly surroundings, Jean, who shared a small room with her two sisters, says she came out of the womb wanting to clean and organize. She couldn't stand staring across her room at her sisters' collective mess, so she resourcefully fashioned a makeshift partition out of wood she found in the basement.

Jean was always driven and decisive. Her goal was to be a beauty executive, so she studied business, finance, and marketing in college. While still in school, she landed an internship in the advertising industry and was offered a paid position right after graduation. Intent on breaking into the fashion industry by any means necessary, Jean started showing up at NYC fashion shows, whether she was invited or not. She threw her energy into building relationships in the industry until she finally was hired by legendary designer Donna Karan. She worked as a marketing executive for luxury products, including pillows, fragrances, candles, and ultimately apparel. It was a competitive environment, but Jean thrived in the industry learning about styling, fitting, and fashion—a childhood dream realized. Jean worked her way up in the industry, including high-level jobs in global marketing with both Estée Lauder and Victoria's Secret, where she met her husband, Michael, who worked in product design and later became a creative director for the brand. Jean spent the next decade attending industry events and fashion shows and traveling the globe, working in Dubai, South America, and across Asia. After the birth of her son, the family outgrew their one bedroom in the West Village and decided to move to Wilton, Connecticut, to be closer to her family and enjoy the spaciousness that life in the suburbs provided. A few years into the brutal commute into the city and the reality of both parents working high-pressure corporate jobs, Jean ultimately made the decision to leave her career to spend more time with her son. She took on consulting work and began dreaming of a new venture—a career as a wardrobe stylist and closet organizer.

Jean had always helped friends and family members clean out their closets and style new outfits, but it never occurred to her that her recreational hobby could become a legitimate career. When her sisters insisted that she should share her talent with the world, she decided to give it a shot,

and her personal-styling and closet-organizing business was born. Her husband designed her logo, a good friend helped create her website, and she used her marketing skills to spread the word about her boutique business. She hit the ground running, researching everything from size-inclusive brands to the best closet-organizing products and created customized packages that included wardrobe editing, personal shopping, styling, and closet organizing. Jean has always been talented at quickly sizing up situations and devising creative solutions, so her new career fit like a glove. She jumped at the chance to help clients clarify their personal style, navigate body-image hang-ups, and reimagine how their closets could look, feel, and function. Jean insisted on helping her clients shop their own closets before adding new items, claiming that most people already owned much of what they needed and that it was often hiding in plain sight, buried in

their overstuffed closets. Although many clients have begged Jean to organize and style other parts of their homes, she prefers to stick with her happy place: the closet.

While Jean's passion for fashion remains, her work is fueled by her desire to build meaningful relationships and make an impact on how women feel in their clothes and in their own skin. She has built a loyal client base in the New York area, and now offers virtual styling services across the United States and internationally in Italy, London, and Dubai. In addition to closet curation and organization, she offers on-demand styling for big trips, parties, and events and is always up for any styling challenge.

She is proud of the business she has built, the flexibility it affords her as a working parent, and the difference it makes in people's day-to-day lives. "Knowing that I'm helping people feel better about themselves is incredible."

JEAN'S HOME

Jean and her husband, Michael, pay attention to the details, as evidenced by their highly curated, contemporary home. Jean jokes that Michael is the art director of the home, while she is the organizer and stylist—a collaboration that's resulted in an elevated aesthetic that even extends to the storage spaces behind closed doors (I peeked!).

The couple teamed up to design and renovate their kitchen—a sleek space with lots of concealed storage so countertops can remain minimal. The living spaces are equally minimal (but comfortable) and accented with bright contemporary art, almost all of it painted by Michael.

Jean's favorite room in the house is her cozy home office, which is furnished with a narrow desk, couch, and coffee table. She keeps her business and office supplies arranged in a small storage closet where her innate sense of style is evident. Office supplies are styled in white and pastel storage boxes, files are tucked away neatly in an acrylic file organizer, and even her camera gear is artfully displayed on a single shelf. The linen closet, typically a bland utilitarian space, is equally lovely to look at. Towels, linens, and blankets in calming, neutral hues are folded in neat stacks, paper goods are removed from plastic and stored in open baskets, and canvas bins contain smaller household essentials, like sunscreen, bug spray, and first-aid supplies.

In the entryway, a floor basket makes a stylish drop station for shoes and boots, jackets are hung in the slim coat closet, and two oversize bins contain seasonal accessories. Given her background in the fashion industry, Jean's weakness for beauty products is no surprise. Her collection is neatly stored in drawer organizers in the bathroom, including a dedicated drawer for travel products and sample sizes for easy packing. A wooden board across the tub provides storage for washcloths, soap, and even a few freshly cut florals, making the bathroom feel more like a spa or a luxury hotel (I'm so in on this concept!).

Jean's background in merchandising and styling was put to good use when she designed her closet and wardrobe area. She created a boutique-inspired space where she displays all her current wardrobe staples (even T-shirts!) in plain sight instead of tucked away in storage boxes or garment bags. Not surprisingly, her closet is carefully curated and displayed so she can get dressed with ease. Off-season items are stored in bins with cedar or lavender for freshness and rotate in as the seasons shift, a practice akin to revisiting old friends. "Hello, cozy scarf. Nice to see you again, summer maxi dress."

Jean treats her closet more like a living space than a storage area. Accents such as scented candles, essential oils, and freshly cut flowers engage the senses, while perfume, jewelry, and memorabilia are stored in pretty boxes and decorative trays. Her favorite necklaces are contained in a shallow drawer with custom dividers to prevent tangling.

Jean is a big believer in investing in fewer, better things and taking care of them, so she keeps a sweater shaver, lint roller, and sewing kit in her closet to keep her wardrobe looking sharp. In her bedroom, a dresser stores folded scarves, loungewear, underwear, pajamas, and workout gear. She likes to stagger her folded items instead of stacking them in a pile, so all items are visible.

Despite her love of fashion and aesthetics, Jean is committed to creating practical, functional systems and strives to merge form and function both in her work with clients and throughout her own home. I'd say she's nailed it.

TIPS + TAKEAWAYS

- Style your wardrobe like an inviting boutique. Jean prefers shoes out of boxes, clothing displayed at arm's reach, and little personal touches such as candles, perfume, and freshly cut flowers. Invest in sturdy, matching hangers and space them evenly for a cohesive look.

- Preserve the shape of your structured handbags by lining them up on a shelf (instead of hanging) and stuffing them with "purse pillows" (this is an actual thing) or even old T-shirts or garment bags.

- Get crafty! Jean cuts pool noodles (in black, of course) to make her own boot shapers in the perfect height.

- Repair before replacing: Keep a sweater shaver, sewing kit, and lint roller in an accessible place in your closet to make it easier to maintain clothing in tip-top shape and ensure maximum use out of each item.

- Wardrobe planning tip: Jean likes to use a small valet rod or garment rack to stage outfits in advance. She also suggests snapping photos of favorite outfit formulas and making an album for visual styling reminders.

Q/A WITH JEAN GORDON

BIGGEST PERSONAL HOME-ORGANIZING CHALLENGE?

I'm happiest when my living space looks pristine and untouched (which is completely unrealistic), so balancing my ideal home aesthetic with daily family functioning is my greatest organizing challenge.

WHAT ARE YOU MOST PROUD OF?

That I combined my fashion and beauty industry experience with my love of creating order to launch my career as a personal stylist and closet organizer.

FAVORITE SPACE TO ORGANIZE?

Closet.

DIRTY LITTLE CLUTTER SECRET? ANY AREAS OF YOUR HOME THAT ARE NOT ORGANIZED?

Under the sink in my kitchen (cleaning supplies and such) can always use a bit of straightening. I use them so often that I haphazardly toss them back in the cabinet.

WHAT IS YOUR MOST TREASURED POSSESSION?

A delicate, gold necklace. Not the fanciest, but sentimental and unique, just like its original owner (my mom).

GREATEST SPLURGE OR EXTRAVAGANCE?

I find it most rewarding when I can plan a fun and slightly indulgent vacation for my family. It's one of the biggest reasons I work so hard.

FAVORITE ORGANIZING HACK?

Using S hooks to hang jeans.

MOST COMMON MISCONCEPTION ABOUT PRO ORGANIZERS?

That organizers are cleaners, when actually we help with the psychology of clutter.

GO-TO DAILY UNIFORM?

Vintage Levi's, white or black T-shirt, tailored coat or jacket, and a pair of hoop earrings.

WHEN YOU'RE NOT ORGANIZING, YOU'RE PROBABLY . . .

Obsessing over fashion. I generally keep it simple when it comes to fashion, but I'm always inspired by fashion week and the street-style moments that accompany it. I love translating innovative styling to more practical everyday wear. I'm also teaching myself how to sew.

ONE SELF-CARE TIP YOU FOLLOW?

Maintaining my small closet-style sanctuary, which is a calm and stress-free place to begin and end each day. It consists of a perfectly edited and organized wardrobe that is shoppable and personal touches that beautify the space: a small vase of fresh flowers and my essential-oil stone diffuser get refreshed regularly.

THE MOST VALUABLE CAREER ADVICE YOU'VE EVER BEEN GIVEN?

Estée Lauder spoke at my college graduation and commencement ceremony. One thing she said resonated: "We learn too much every day to settle for yesterday's achievements." Never forgot it. It keeps me curious and motivates me to continue pushing forward, even when I'm tired.

A RISK YOU TOOK THAT PAID OFF?

Went skydiving on a first date. Ended up marrying him.

FAVORITE GIFT TO GIVE?

I love giving a unique fashion accessory that my friends or family wouldn't typically buy for themselves but would have fun wearing. It's a great pick-me-up.

WHAT MIGHT PEOPLE BE SURPRISED TO LEARN ABOUT YOU?

I worked on a freestyle–house music dance album while in college. It climbed to number four on the dance charts!

THE ENTREPRENEUR'S STYLISH LOFT

ASHLEY'S STORY

There are many professional organizers who never imagined they'd be tidying professionally, but Ashley Jones had a particularly winding path to her organizing career. She credits her mother—who had a military background and never went to bed until the kitchen was spotless—with teaching her the importance of a tidy home.

After graduating from college with degrees in fashion merchandising, apparel design, and marketing, Ashley taught for the Princeton Review and was their ACT Master Trainer while she was in graduate school. But her love of fashion led her to a development and production job with Ralph Lauren in New York City, and later to a fashion teaching position at the Art Institute of Washington.

Ashley was next tapped to help launch and open a bakery franchise. She found herself putting her business education to use and quickly taught herself how to obtain permits, read blueprints, and oversee the entire development process of opening a retail business, including construction and pre-opening operational activities. *Competent* is her middle name.

After successfully opening the bakery, Ashley caught the entrepreneurial bug. When she learned that Neat Method (see pages 49–51), a popular home-organizing company, had a franchise opportunity open in her area, she jumped at the chance. While Ashley had no experience as a home organizer, she was confident she could draw on relevant experience from her background in fashion and merchandising, business operations, and management. Ashley landed her first big organizing job quickly: a huge move-in project, which she knew she couldn't tackle alone. After scrambling to borrow staff from the bakery to help unpack and set up the entire home, her team was met with rave reviews and her business was officially launched.

Ashley quickly discovered that her experience in fashion and her understanding of blueprints and buildouts made her uniquely qualified to design luxury closets and customized pantries, mudrooms, and garages for her clients—and these luxury services became her specialty. She loved designing practical but glamorous spaces with "a little touch of sexy."

Not one to miss a great event, Ashley attended many social gatherings where she had opportunities to network. She credits her ability to connect with others with her early and steady business success.

While entrepreneurship can be a lonely path, Ashley had company as part of Neat Method's close-knit franchise community of female entrepreneurs. After five successful years running her own business, Ashley was offered the role of director of franchise development for Neat Method. In her new role, Ashley ensured that the company had solid systems in place to support other Neat Method franchise owners with education and training, resources, and growth opportunities. She became the organizer behind a nationwide network of organizers. It didn't take long for Ashley to be promoted to a new position: chief growth officer. In this role, she worked directly with all the franchise owners, managing the growth and development of all ninety-five professional-organizing franchises in the company. She was also selected to represent the company nationally for press opportunities and became the spokesperson for the brand on *The Today Show,* where she has shared home-organizing demos and expert tips.

After more than six years of supporting the team at Neat Method, Ashley pivoted again and decided to launch her own new venture: a boutique consultancy designed to support other entrepreneurs in a range of fields. A creative with an eye for detail, Ashley brings her charming personality and strong leadership skills to every venture she takes on, with organization as the foundation of every project.

ASHLEY'S HOME

Ashley's sunny loft practically screams, "A professional organizer lives here!" All household essentials are grouped by type and stored neatly in stylish, matching bins, labeled with her impeccable handwriting (it looks like a font—Ashley, teach me your ways!).

Ashley lives in a lively neighborhood full of great restaurants and admits she rarely cooks, but that hasn't stopped her from meticulously organizing every square inch of her kitchen. A small countertop organizer contains salt, pepper, oven mitts, and frequently used kitchen tools, while spices are decanted into matching clear jars and lined up in a wall-mounted organizer. Everything from medicines, smoothie ingredients, condiments, and cooking oils are stowed in clear, labeled bins and tucked out of sight in a cabinet. Ashley has also created an inviting makeshift pantry using nothing more than a set of eight pull-out bins arranged neatly on five narrow shelves. She

uses magnetic chalkboard labels from the Neat Method product line to categorize all her staples, including beans, grains, pasta, spice kits, breakfast basics, bars, and snacks.

Since her cabinet space is limited, Ashley has become an expert at stacking and nesting. She proudly shares that she's found a way to stack thirty-six glasses in just nineteen inches of space, and her food storage containers and measuring cups nest perfectly into neat space-saving stacks. She even has a collapsible funnel. Who knew this was a thing? Now we all do.

Her fun style and personality, along with simple, logical systems, are infused into every room in this home. Kitchen gadgets and utensils are bright and stylish (she cites Food52 as a favorite source), and she sprinkles personal touches in each room, like the framed maps that represent every state she's ever lived in. In the living room, all the household remotes are stored together vertically in a repurposed utensil container to avoid getting misplaced. Discarding packaging and decanting products, like sugar and flour, into matching vessels is a common organizing practice in a kitchen, but Ashley has taken it a step further, decanting her board game pieces into clear, labeled canisters to make them more accessible and inviting (the game boards and instructions are stored flat in a drawer just below). This easy hack turns game pieces into eye candy and also saves space without large and multi-size game boxes. Bonus: No more dusty, busted cardboard boxes.

Ashley has always been interested in style and fashion, and her closet is a tribute to the styles and brands she loves most. She personally removed the wire shelving that came with the rental unit and replaced it with a custom closet system she designed herself. Bonus: The system is easily removable and completely portable, making it a great investment for renters. The impressive "wall of footwear" would make any shoe lover swoon, and Ashley's equally impressive baseball hat collection is proudly displayed

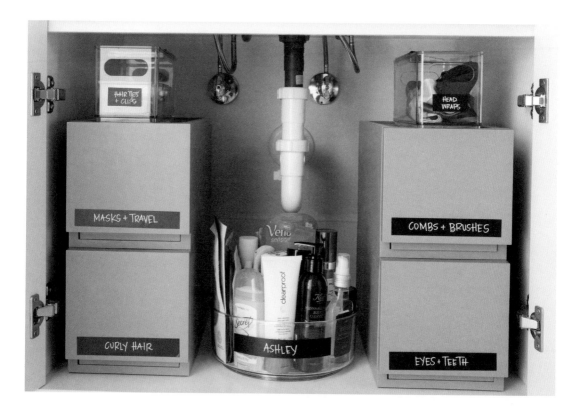

on the top shelf. Her clothing is organized by both type and color and her background in fashion and merchandising is evident in her thoughtful styling—the whole space feels like a boutique. Open labeled bins neatly contain belts, swimsuits, and other accessories, while a sleek acrylic organizer makes it easy to vertically "file" her favorite clutches, wallets, and pouches.

Having traveled and moved frequently, Ashley is now a pro at shopping for furniture with storage and organization in mind. In her home office, she invested in a desk with enough drawer capacity to house all her office supplies and files, and she maximized vertical space above the desk using a modular wall-mounted shelving system to display books, reference materials, art supplies, and inspiration. On the opposite wall, a bookshelf holds her favorite fashion books alongside all her craft and sewing supplies in brightly patterned boxes. A small organizer with mini labeled drawers contains all the tiny supplies such as buttons and needles, while rolls of thread are organized by color in clear canisters, resembling an art installation. She's expertly transformed the back of her entry coat closet into a gift-wrap station (complete with scissors, tape, ribbon, paper, gift tags, and bags) by mounting a hanging organizing system. To account for the absence of a proper linen closet, Ashley added a wall of shelving in the back of her bedroom closet to create her own. Without an attic, basement, or garage, she's created clever systems throughout the home, citing the easy-to-install Elfa modular systems as a favorite for personal and client use alike.

Ashley is one of the few pro organizers who dared to let us snap a photo under her bathroom sink—awkward pipe and all! She's brilliantly transformed the tight space into a functional storage area by using compact stackable drawers to contain products and toiletries. The drawer system makes it easy to access products without any hunting or rearranging, and a small turntable displays daily-use products so she can keep counters clear and clean.

While Ashley confesses that she used to let mail, dirty clothes, dry cleaning, and kitchen glasses linger and pile up, she now implements the "one touch rule" as much as possible to keep her home feeling good: once she uses something, she forces herself to put it away immediately in its designated place. This simple practice ensures that she never has to face a massive clean-up (or a mountain of clutter) at the end of each day. Ashley claims she is more type B than type A, but her use of practical systems, smart storage, and great habits make her home an organizer's dream.

TIPS + TAKEAWAYS

- Unbox your puzzles and games: Ashley decants game pieces into clear vessels and stores gameboards below in a single drawer to maximize space.

- Optimize your walls for storage: modular wall-mounted storage maximizes vertical space and creates storage anywhere it's needed.

- Wrap it up! Repurpose the back of a door to make a sleek and stylish gift-wrapping station.

- Nest and stack food storage, glassware, and bowls to maximize storage space in your kitchen.

- Add personality to daily-use utilitarian items—Ashley loves utensils and kitchen gadgets in bold colors and fun styles.

- Framing maps of the places you've lived is a fun way to personalize your home.

- Practice the "one touch rule" to keep your home looking sharp. Don't put it down, put it away.

Q/A WITH ASHLEY JONES

BIGGEST HOME-ORGANIZING CHALLENGE?
My coat closet. It acts as a storage area for coats, travel, gift wrap, cleaning supplies, and general items.

WHAT ARE YOU MOST PROUD OF?
The quality of work I produce. It requires a lot of hard work and extreme attention to detail, but whatever I tackle, I take pride in knowing I've created a space or business work product that is both beautiful and functional.

FAVORITE SPACE TO ORGANIZE?
Closets because they are an integration of my love of fashion with spatial planning and organizing.

DIRTY LITTLE CLUTTER SECRET?
My home office! It serves as my workspace, workout area, sewing storage, and guest sleeping space. When a space serves so many functions, it can be hard to keep it together all the time.

CAN'T-LIVE-WITHOUT ORGANIZING PRODUCT?
Chalkboard labels. Labels can often feel so permanent, so I love using erasable chalk markers, especially in pantries and kids' rooms.

MOST TREASURED POSSESSION?
My mother's military flag.

GREATEST EXTRAVAGANCE?
I've got a pricey Zimmermann dress habit that I can't seem to kick.

MOST COMMON MISCONCEPTION ABOUT PRO ORGANIZERS?
That we are cleaners (or maids). That we will make you throw it all away. That we have a one-size-fits-all approach for all homes. That we all have perfect homes. That we are always judging others for not being organized.

BIGGEST TAKEAWAY OR LESSON LEARNED FROM ORGANIZING OTHER PEOPLE'S HOMES?
Keep only what you use or wear. So often, people hold on to items for those "just in case" moments that may never happen. I have found that when they do happen, for example if you're invited to a fancy gala, you'll likely want something new anyway.

WHEN YOU'RE NOT ORGANIZING, YOU'RE PROBABLY . . .
Traveling to visit friends and cool boutique hotels, drinking spicy margaritas, or catching up on my favorite TV shows.

ACTUAL MORNING ROUTINE?
A quick email and calendar check before getting out of bed, a three-minute skincare routine, and coffee. I wake up earlier when I have a full plate so I can have uninterrupted time to myself.

ACTUAL EVENING ROUTINE?
I like to end the night with a funny movie (I'm a sucker for rom-coms and will rewatch movies I love a hundred times) or a lighthearted show to relax my mind from the day. I'm also obsessed with Bamford's B Silent Night-Time Pillow Mist and give my pillow three sprays every night before bed. I swear it makes me sleep better.

ONE SELF-CARE TIP YOU FOLLOW?
Frequent massages (organizing is labor intensive and can be taxing on your body).

THE MOST VALUABLE CAREER ADVICE YOU'VE EVER BEEN GIVEN?
Take the time to fill your own cup first because that will give you the energy and creativity you need to show up properly for others.

HOLLY BLAKEY

A LIGHT AND AIRY
CALIFORNIA RANCHER

HOLLY'S STORY

Born in New Mexico, Holly's family moved to the San Francisco Bay Area when she was four years old. Holly describes herself as an energetic and social but highly sensitive child who relied heavily on her environment to recharge. An empath to the fullest degree, she was always looking after others and remembers a few early elementary years where she would spend her recess ensuring that nobody was being bullied on the schoolyard. When the outside world felt overwhelming, she found solace in her room, a space she loved rearranging, decorating, and, of course, organizing to create inner calm. She laughs while recalling that she would gift her friends items to spruce up their rooms instead of toys for their birthdays—which was occasionally met with blank stares.

Holly's strong desire to help others coupled with her interest in understanding the human brain led her to pursue a degree in cognitive psychology. As part of her program, she spent four years working closely with autistic children, and her work gave great insight into how clutter and environment affect children with disabilities: when there was less external stimulation and a space was organized and designed for predictability, the kids became noticeably calmer. She loved using her innate skillset of creating order and organization to help support the children she worked with.

Following college graduation, Holly traveled extensively and landed a job as a fashion and travel editor for a Southern California–based magazine. While the job had its perks (hello, NY fashion week!), the glamorous and action-packed lifestyle wasn't for Holly, who was happiest at home, curled up in her cozy sweats. A move back to San Francisco with her boyfriend (now husband), Ben, prompted her to pivot to a corporate marketing and PR job in the tech industry. While she always enjoyed the connections she formed with coworkers and clients, she intuitively knew she couldn't sustain the high-intensity pace for an industry that she wasn't passionate about. (Cloud storage? She was way more excited about closet storage.) During her lunch breaks, she would wander over to the Container Store to browse products and revel in the neatly stacked rows of color-coded containers. She was the first woman in her company to become pregnant, and while her team was supportive, her maternity leave acted as a pause to reassess the woman and mom she wanted to be going forward. While she enjoyed a break from the fast pace and

long hours, having a new baby, no set hours, no pats on the back for a job well done, and post-partum anxiety left her feeling lost. She wanted to contribute to her family and find a career that felt like an authentic fit, but she didn't know where to start. Everything changed when a mentor asked her, "What would you do for fun and for free?" The answer came to her in an instant: giving others a sense of "breathing room" by creating organized spaces.

Once the "ding, ding, ding!" moment occurred, it didn't take long for Holly to start building out a business plan, meeting with veteran organizers in the city, diving into brand development, and booking local friends, family, and neighbors. Equipped with nothing but her love of organizing, Holly faced a healthy dose of imposter syndrome, but she built confidence with each new project, and the work itself felt like an instant and perfect fit. As Holly's family grew (she now has three young children), so did her client load, which consists primarily of other busy, working moms looking for support to ease the stress of managing a household while juggling a career. Clients and fans alike are drawn to Holly's sweet disposition, and her talent for creating stylish, functional, and family-friendly spaces. Reducing overwhelm and putting a smile on other people's faces remains an integral part of her mission. As Holly says, "Helping to lighten another mom's load feels endlessly fulfilling."

HOLLY'S HOME

The 1952 rancher Holly shares with her husband and three young children is a study in brilliant, concealed storage. Aware firsthand how overwhelming visual clutter can be for kids and adults alike, Holly's renovation and design decisions prioritized integrating discreet and practical storage solutions into every room.

The small entry closet opens to reveal a neat row of labeled bins that store umbrellas, hats, scarves, masks, and other family essentials, while an oversize floor basket (deep enough to conceal its contents) sits beside the closet, so the kids can easily toss their backpacks when they arrive home from school. Also near the front door, a small linen closet doubles as a well-stocked utility station. Holly has centralized all the family's frequent grab-and-go essentials in open bins that are conveniently at arm's reach: sunscreen, Band-Aids, first-aid supplies, cough and cold remedies, travel-size products, diapers and wipes, and paper products.

In the bathrooms, wooden drawer dividers keep products tidy. In the kids' shared bathroom, Holly designed a low drawer beneath the sink with a pull-out sturdy step stool for the children. Now I want a secret drawer-stool! Holly describes herself as obsessive when it comes to clean lines. Her home office has been integrated into her bedroom, but to minimize visual distraction, all office supplies, notebooks, and reference materials are organized in matching white storage containers stacked up neatly behind closed doors.

In the kitchen Holly has dedicated a deep drawer for containing the art and finished homework the three kids bring home from school each day. Instead of floating around the home and cluttering up the counters, each child has their own designated drawer. At the end of each month, Holly helps them sort through and pick their favorites so they can recycle the rest and start fresh (Holly turns the selected favorites into special keepsake art books—a pro tip).

The kitchen has ample storage so counters can remain clean and clear. All appliances in the home are stored inside cabinets with custom outlets so distracting cords are out of sight (shout out to a microwave concealed in a drawer—I'm clearly taking notes of this innovation for my own home!). Vitamins, supplements, medicines, and protein powders are organized in labeled bins and turntables on a high shelf, and clutter culprits, like kid lunch boxes and water bottles, are rinsed and placed in a deep drawer when the school day is done.

Holly's fridge is a work of art (yes, it really does look like this on the regular), which she attributes to buying just what she needs each week, ditching all packaging, and having a small, bonus fridge where she can house backstock. Eggs, produce, and leftovers are stored in reusable containers (no plastic berry baskets, egg crates, or plastic wrap found here!), and herbs are kept fresh in narrow tumblers with water. Holly admits that, like me, she's a sucker for good packaging (and quality ingredients!), and I observe that even her oat milk and yogurt containers are lovely to look at (prompting me to go home and completely overhaul my own fridge, which my kids have filled with tinfoil balls of mystery foods).

Her food-wraps drawer (an oft neglected zone) is equally easy on the eyes. Holly has tracked down functional alternatives to plastic, and stores her biodegradable snack, sandwich, and freezer bags, as well as aluminum foil, in sleek wooden organizers, creating a streamlined and cohesive aesthetic. When she shared this drawer on social media, it went viral.

Holly designed and customized the small pantry like a beautifully curated gourmet foods shop. She painted the shelves a crisp bright white and maximized space by decanting all baking staples into clear jars with wooden tops. The rest of the shelves are organized with uniform labeled bins for corralling snacks and family staples. I quickly learn that Holly takes snacking seriously. Within a span of five minutes, she introduces me to tasty gluten-free corn crisp crackers, granola that tastes like pancakes with maple syrup, and a delicious mint-chip smoothie made from spinach and banana. Notes are taken for future snack purchases.

In the adjacent family room, built-in cabinets conceal the kids' arts and crafts, as well as the family's electronics, cords, printer, and paper. Everything has a place, and all supplies are tucked away neatly behind closed doors. Living a clutter-free life with three young kids is no easy feat, but Holly makes it seem achievable through her clever use of concealed storage and good habits, like a quick tidy before bed. She jokes, "I'm not always the most organized, but I'm really good at hiding things."

Holly knows that kids do better with less stuff and less stimulation, and she focuses on purchasing a few meaningful and experiential gifts for birthdays and holidays, so there's less stuff to keep up with and manage. Games, toys, books, and stuffed animals are stored in their respective closets to ensure that their bedrooms remain less stimulating for story time and sleep. Fueled by the belief that kids thrive with predictable order, Holly makes sure to involve her kids in organizing their things and taking ownership over the upkeep of their own spaces. She has also implemented a simple hack she dubbed the "transitional basket" to corral any items that tend to pile up throughout the day. She'll toss in any random items the kids have left out, and at the end of the day she'll take a few minutes to relocate everything.

With clean lines, smart systems, and loads of customized storage, this busy family home truly has a place for everything. Holly has created a bright, stylish, and inviting space with plenty of breathing room for her friends and family to gather, play, eat, and relax.

TIPS + TAKEAWAYS

- Ditch the packaging! Holly removes all packaging and stores products in elevated vessels, like glass jars or open bins.

- Especially for kids who are sensitive, store toys, games, and stuffed animals in open vessels made of soft, quiet fabrics such as cotton or felt.

- Corral medicines, vitamins, and supplements into turntables, and set up your "wellness station" in a cool, dry place that young kids can't reach or access.

- Centralize frequent-use products, like sunscreen, Band-Aids, and paper goods, into your own personal general store for easy grab-and-go access.

- If you have commitment issues with hanging art, use Command hooks instead of nails.

- Try a transitional basket. If you hate the feeling of tidying all day, toss random items into a designated basket and relocate when you have time.

- Treat yourself! When it comes to snack time, pay attention to both ingredients and good packaging. Store products by type in open bins for easy snacking. I'm off to track down that maple syrup granola . . .

Q/A WITH HOLLY BLAKEY

BIGGEST PERSONAL HOME-ORGANIZING CHALLENGE?
Three kids who love stuff.

WHAT ARE YOU MOST PROUD OF?
Seeing my kids be kind to others when they don't know I'm watching. There's nothing better.

DIRTY LITTLE CLUTTER SECRET?
My car is always a hot mess . . . don't even look at the car seats.

MOST TREASURED POSSESSION?
A vintage Rolex bracelet that belonged to my great-grandmother and my grandmother's beaded veil headpiece—my wedding bouquet was wrapped in it.

FAVORITE ORGANIZING HACK?
Can I say "donation center"? Ha!

WHAT DO YOU DO WHEN YOU FEEL OVERWHELMED IN A HOME OR SPACE?
Start sorting . . . you have to just start.

MOST COMMON MISCONCEPTION ABOUT PRO ORGANIZERS?
That we color coordinate our snacks.

BEST ADVICE FOR ASPIRING ENTREPRENEURS?
Just try. Find people who can be your cheerleaders and go for it!

BIGGEST TAKEAWAY OR LESSON LEARNED FROM ORGANIZING OTHER PEOPLE'S HOMES?
You have to listen. Each client is so different.

WHEN YOU'RE NOT ORGANIZING, YOU'RE PROBABLY . . .
Spending time with my kids, doing yoga, and sending extra-long voice memos to my best girlfriends.

ACTUAL MORNING ROUTINE?
When things go according to plan: wake up at 5:45 and either take a yoga class or make my matcha, do morning pages (from *The Artist's Way*) for twenty minutes, then jump into the craziness of three kids before school.

ACTUAL EVENING ROUTINE?
I sit on the couch with my husband and do work for one to two hours while he watches TV (and I pretend to watch), then read in bed until I fall asleep.

THE MOST VALUABLE CAREER ADVICE YOU'VE EVER BEEN GIVEN?
"Sometimes you have to spend money to make money." That was a hard one for me to accept.

A RISK YOU TOOK THAT PAID OFF?
Hiring a nanny. When I was first getting started, I believed I shouldn't pay for help if I wasn't making a lot of money. But I couldn't actually work if I didn't have help. Our nanny of five years was the biggest risk (for me as a mom with little ones), and the best investment.

FAVORITE GIFT TO GIVE?
Beautiful flowers or a yummy treat. I like gifting things that don't create clutter.

WHAT KIND OF PLANNER DO YOU USE? HOW DO YOU ORGANIZE YOUR DAY?
Sugar Paper planner. Each night I look at my schedule for the next day and list the top three priority action items. Those come first. If I can get to more, great—but I've learned not to overwhelm myself.

GO-TO DAILY UNIFORM?
Ripped jeans and a vintage T-shirt with a big, cozy sweater.

CLAUDIA TORRE

TREETOP VIEWS IN THE HEART OF MÉXICO CITY

CLAUDIA'S STORY

One of the first things I learned about Claudia was that she has moved forty-six times in her life. The oldest of three siblings, Claudia was born in México City and grew up in nearby Cuernavaca, a lush city with a temperate climate once favored by Aztec emperors, princes, and artists. Her free-spirited mother embraced adventure and creativity in all forms: Claudia and her siblings frequently changed paint colors, rearranged furniture, swapped rooms, and even suspended Claudia's bed from the ceiling when she wanted to try something new on a whim (please don't tell my kids this is possible!). After her parents divorced, Claudia's mother often rented out their large home, which was overwhelming to maintain, and the family moved from house to house, changing schools and environments each time. Claudia fully embraced the nomadic lifestyle and always admired how her mother lived life with passion and zest. Years later, when the family was forced to dramatically downsize and sell their home to pay for her mother's cancer treatments, Claudia's mother insisted that they keep the finest plates, mugs, and glasses so every day would still feel like a celebration.

A self-described nerd, Claudia learned English in school as a child, becoming so proficient in the language that she started working as a translator at the age of thirteen. She went on to pursue a degree in media and communications, breaking up her studies with extended trips to Madrid, London, Paris, Vancouver, and Chicago. After receiving her degree, Claudia was hired to work on a cruise ship and spent the next year traveling around the Caribbean and Mediterranean. While her colleagues would go to parties on the ship, she would opt out, preferring to spend her free hours organizing their living quarters. Her friends insisted that she find a way to make a career out of her incredible skill, but when she scoured the internet using the Spanish words for search terms, like *declutter* or *home organizer*, not a single thing came up in the search results. Not one to give up easily, Claudia repeated her search but this time in English. She discovered not only that professional organizing existed as an actual career, but there were even professional associations for the industry across the United States and Canada. Claudia became obsessed, searching the directories and reaching out to every organizer she could find to figure out how she could get started in the field.

Eventually, Claudia's search led her to Marla Dee, a well-established professional organizer in Utah, who had launched a training institute. Claudia whipped through Marla's comprehensive at-home, six-month, self-study course in three weeks, then immediately enrolled in the next in-person certification program in Utah. After completing her certification, she returned to México City eager to launch her new home-organizing business, but when she talked about her services, she was met with confusion and blank stares. This was 2011, and the home-organizing craze had not yet hit México.

Deflated but not defeated, Claudia channeled her passion for organizing into a lifestyle blog, documenting everything that she had learned about decluttering and living better with less. After two years of posting consistently, she got a call from one of the biggest national television networks in México. They were excited by what she was sharing and invited her to have a regular segment on the national television show *Ellas Arriba*, teaching organization to viewers. Her visibility also landed her a regular spot on the wildly popular Martha Debayle national radio show. As Claudia's profile grew, she suddenly became a pioneer and a trailblazer for the home-organizing

industry in a place where it hadn't previously existed. It wasn't long before she was flooded with emails from people all over Latin America who wanted to learn from her and get certified. At that time there wasn't a single certification program for home organizers that was taught in Spanish. Moved by the intense level of demand, Claudia finally relented, compiled everything she had learned into a 250-page training manual, and in 2015 launched an academy to train new organizers in Spanish. Hundreds of people flocked to México City to train with her, including students from Chile, Colombia, El Salvador, Ecuador, Peru, Uruguay, and Spain, as well as Canada and the United States. Claudia established a reputation for leading dynamic training intensives where students would have the opportunity to organize an entire home, under her supervision, in a single weekend. Like so many other businesses, the pandemic forced Claudia to pivot and offer her training program online, and her students used her methodology to completely transform their own homes.

In addition to the thriving academy and her home-organizing business, Claudia also launched her own product line to fill gaps in the marketplace, which she sells exclusively to her clients. With a book in the works that will document her personal journey and business methodology, Claudia's thriving career shows no sign of slowing down. As she tells me with a smile, "I know I can achieve anything I put my mind to."

CLAUDIA'S HOME

Claudia's two-bedroom apartment is located on a beautiful tree-lined street in the Polanco neighborhood of México City, surrounded by parks, cafés, and restaurants. Her home is impeccably tidy and organized but still manages to feel warm and welcoming, just like Claudia herself, who greets Vivian and me with squeals from the window when we arrive. Claudia clearly takes pride in her home, and the freshly painted walls are accented with items full of personal meaning—there's the colorful dream catcher that her Colombian student made her; the framed black-and-white snapshot of her hands entwined with her mother's, moments before she lost her to cancer (this caused me to burst into tears on the spot); the jewelry organizer she constructed herself out of old corks; and her personal mantra propped up in a frame: "Si necesitas creer en algo, cree en ti" ("If you need to believe in something, believe in yourself"). As she shows me around her home, I am struck by her meticulous level of organization. Her office and scrapbooking supplies are arranged neatly in drawers with dividers to separate each item. Work binders are lined up in neat rows on her office shelves. Spices have been decanted and labeled. Her colorful scarf collection is arranged in rainbow order, and each one is file-folded so precisely in her drawer that I have to reach out and touch them to make sure they're real (they are). When I sneak a peek of Claudia putting away her laundry, I am mesmerized by the patience with which she folds her socks in precise little packages and lines them up in her drawers. The level of care and concentration feels almost spiritual. Note: Not all organizers (raising my hand, here) possess this superhuman level of patience or attention to detail.

Claudia is a natural-born problem solver, and she uses her newly launched line of organizing products throughout her home to optimize and organize her space: the hanging travel bag with detachable pouches, the sleek pill-and-medicine organizer, the packing cubes tucked away in her suitcase, and the purse-organizing insert she uses to keep her handbag tidy.

Claudia gravitates toward minimalism and has worked hard to strike just the right balance of owning exactly what she needs without any excess. This effort has paid off and makes it easy to manage and maintain her space, even with her exceptionally busy career and lifestyle. One of Claudia's organizing mantras is "keep only the things you love, use, need, and that make you happy," and her home is a beautiful example of this ethos.

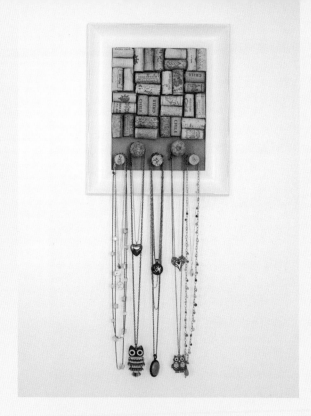

TIPS + TAKEAWAYS

- Give unfinished projects a specific deadline, and put a sticky note with the date of the deadline on each one. If you haven't finished a project by the deadline, then commit to tossing, donating, or giving it away. Bye!

- Identify a great local organization, ideally with a mission you are personally passionate about, to donate your unwanted items to. Claudia brings all her client donations to Casa de la Amistad, a nonprofit that uses proceeds from the resale of donated items to help families cover the cost of treatment for children battling cancer.

- Get crafty: Repurpose household objects to create your own organizing solutions. Claudia made a wall-mounted jewelry organizer, which she uses and loves, by removing the glass from an old picture frame and attaching old wine corks with a hot glue gun.

- Create a designated treasure box for safely storing sentimental items and mementos. Honor these meaningful keepsakes in their own safe and guarded place.

Q/A WITH CLAUDIA TORRE

WHAT DO YOU LOVE MOST ABOUT YOUR HOME?
It's cozy. I love the Danish hygge way of life, and I try to live by it. Comfy couch, soft blankets, hot beverages, and lit scented candles.

BIGGEST HOME-ORGANIZING CHALLENGE?
I lost my apartment in the terrible earthquake that struck México City in 2017. I had to find another place with whatever remained that was salvageable, and because it was a shocking and unexpected moment, it took months for me to recover. I even had to hire my own assistant to be my professional organizer as I regained my peace of mind and set up my new space.

WHAT ARE YOU THE PROUDEST OF?
I was the first professional organizer in México, when the industry didn't exist in the country. I was a pioneer. I built my business from nothing. It has become an institution in Latin America, all in the course of ten years. I launched the first Spanish-language Professional Organizing Academy and built a community of hundreds of women who have turned their passion into their profession.

CAN'T-LIVE-WITHOUT ORGANIZING PRODUCT?
My purse organizer, but a close second is a good scrapbook. I have a scrapbook collection of every year of my life, made by me!

BIGGEST TAKEAWAY OR LESSON LEARNED FROM ORGANIZING OTHER PEOPLE'S HOMES?
It's not about the stuff, it's about the person. We deal with human beings in pain—who often feel overwhelmed, lost, and vulnerable. When you focus on the person, the stuff just floats away.

WHAT DOES SELF-CARE LOOK LIKE FOR YOU?
Being kind to yourself. Respecting hours of sleep, healthy eating, and pampering yourself. Positive thoughts that nurture your soul. Consuming books, videos, and audio that make you a better version of yourself.

WHAT DO YOU DO WHEN YOU FEEL OVERWHELMED IN A HOME OR SPACE?
Follow the steps of my methodology (La Metodología del O.R.D.E.N.)

Ordena: Categorize and sort like with like

Reduce: Declutter your possessions

Da un hogar: Assign each item a home

Etiqueta: Find the perfect container and label

¡No Recaigas!: Maintain your work

I know that by following these steps I will finish the project successfully.

MOST COMMON MISCONCEPTION ABOUT PRO ORGANIZERS?
They're only for celebrities and rich people.

YOUR DEFINITION OF ORGANIZED?
To have only the things you love, use, need, and that make you happy, so you can focus on what really matters—more experiences, not more things.

THE MOST VALUABLE CAREER ADVICE YOU'VE EVER BEEN GIVEN?
Surround yourself with successful people that you look up to. Talk to them, learn from them and their experience. Read about them, listen to podcasts, audiobooks, watch documentaries about their lives. Put yourself in the same frequency.

A RISK YOU TOOK THAT PAID OFF?
Flying to Salt Lake City and getting certified. It was a different country with a whole new career path, but it gave me the tools, knowledge, and confidence to believe in myself and create a ten-plus-year business that got me to where I am today.

WHAT MIGHT PEOPLE BE SURPRISED TO LEARN ABOUT YOU?
People think I'm extroverted, but I love to be by myself. I really enjoy my *me time.* I enjoy *silence*, and I have never been *bored* a day in my life.

A small space doesn't have to feel like a big sacrifice. A home with a smaller footprint is better for the environment, better for your bank account, and can even help facilitate a more active and creative life. But despite the many perks, small-space living is sure to come with some challenges. If you're a fellow small-space dweller, read on for some of my favorite space-maximizing solutions.

GO VERTICAL

Need more storage space? Look up! Installing extra shelves that extend from the floor to the ceiling can maximize your space like nothing else. In the closet, extra shelves and rods can come in handy, and in the kitchen, storage cabinets can be installed all the way to the ceiling for a more customized look.

WALL LEDGES FOR THE WIN

A single wall shelf (or art ledge) can be a game changer when it comes to storage in a small space. These narrow shelves take a few screws to install and work wonders for storing products, plants, decor, spices, books, art, folded towels—you name it!

NEST FOR SUCCESS

Luggage can be a beast to store when you're short on space. If you have more than one suitcase, try nesting them together like Matryoshka dolls (you can also store seasonal items like bulky sweaters or coats in your suitcases). This approach also applies to glassware, food storage containers, mixing bowls, and any other household items that can neatly nest.

HOOKS SOLVE EVERYTHING

Hooks are an organizer's best friend and an easy and affordable way to add additional storage to a small space. A row of hooks is a smart entryway addition for hanging bags, hats, pet leashes, and coats by the front door. Hooks in the kitchen can be used for dish towels, kitchen scissors, cookware, utensils, aprons, and oven mitts. In the bathroom, hooks are ideal for robes, hand and bath towels, and in the closet, hooks can be used for jewelry, hats, and bags.

CONCEAL THE BULKY STUFF

Small homes are often short on storage, so adding a set of narrow cabinets with doors (the Billy from IKEA is a great option) can create additional space for household items you want to contain and conceal, such as your printer, vacuum, or electronics. Painting your storage cabinets the same color as your walls can help create a custom look that virtually disappears.

INVEST IN DUAL-PURPOSE PRODUCTS

When space is not on your side, invest in products that can serve multiple functions, like a toaster oven that's also an air fryer, or a washer-dryer combo. It also makes sense to invest in convertible furniture whenever possible—a stool that can double as a nightstand, a bench or coffee table with concealed storage, a bed with built-in drawers for linens or clothing—you get the picture.

TRY A CAPSULE WARDROBE

Creating a pared-down wardrobe (or even a daily uniform) consisting of versatile mix-and-match pieces will not only create breathing room in your closet, but it will also reduce stress and decision fatigue; save you time, money, and energy; and (big bonus!) it's better for the planet.

SHARING IS CARING

All for one and one for all! A single shampoo, conditioner, bodywash, or even (gasp) toothpaste, can go a long way in maximizing space in a tiny, shared bathroom.

PICK ONE

Pare down your collections to the best and the brightest of the bunch. If you have ten black sweaters, pick your favorites. If you're storing your grandmother's china set that you never use, keep one teacup to treasure. Own five umbrellas that you always misplace? Choose one and store it in a designated spot. Keeping just one item from a collection will free up valuable real estate in your home and make the items you keep feel more special.

DO YOU REALLY NEED THAT ____?

It took a kitchen remodel that greatly reduced our storage for our family to realize we could happily survive without a (trigger warning!) microwave. Our bulky salad spinner, dish rack, and panini press also hit the road. If storage is not on your side, consider what you use and need on the regular, and let the rest go.

BORROW INSTEAD OF BUYING

We live in a sharing economy, and it's now much easier to rent or borrow the things you need instead of buying them. Baby gear, sports and camping equipment, appliances, specialty tools, formal attire—you name it, there's a service (or a friendly neighbor) that can lend or rent it to you.

BANISH THE BACKSTOCK

Ever heard the expression "store it at the store"? It's a favorite around here. If your home is tight on storage, buy what you need and replenish as necessary.

STORE IT WHERE YOU USE IT

For especially small dwellings, it can be handy to store things where you use them. Use your toaster oven as a makeshift breadbox and tuck your weekly loaf inside (just make sure you remove it if you're going to make toast!). Large pots or pans can rest on your stovetop or even inside your oven. Plates and bowls can be stacked neatly on your countertop if you don't have a cabinet to spare.

EMPLOY PRINCIPLES OF MINIMALISM

Obvious as it sounds, owning less stuff is the most direct route to creating more space in a small home. Be intentional about the things you buy, and make sure the items you bring into your home are truly worth the space they take up.

5 REASONS I DON'T WANT A BIGGER HOME

Time for some real talk. Most people want a bigger house. I don't. Our home is 1,200 square feet, which feels absolutely perfect for our busy family of four, plus one furry friend. Here's why I think less equates to so much more . . .

FINANCIAL FREEDOM

Having a home with a smaller footprint means a smaller monthly payment for mortgage, taxes, and insurance. Because we have chosen to live within our means, we don't feel the financial strain that comes with investing in a bigger or more impressive plot of real estate. Living small means we need less of literally everything (house paint, tools, cleaning products, furniture, organizing products—you name it!). Being able to comfortably pay for our home and maintain it leads to less overall stress and relationship strain and frees up resources we can use toward eating out, travel, personal development, and philanthropy.

LESS TO CLEAN AND MAINTAIN

To be perfectly candid, I'm not a fan of cleaning, and there are a million things I would rather do than spend my time on household maintenance and upkeep. A smaller home enables us to spend less time cleaning, decluttering, and organizing, and more time relaxing and enjoying our home and our lives. I'm even relieved we don't have a backyard because the thought of having a lawn to take care of fills me with dread—I can barely keep a houseplant alive.

WE CAN INVEST IN FEWER, BETTER THINGS

Years ago, when we decided to retile our bathroom, I realized that we could afford to pick out any tile we wanted because our single shared bathroom is the size of a small postage stamp. With fewer rooms to furnish, paint, and style, we have the luxury of investing in high-quality products, furniture, and finishes. I also love to splurge on fresh flowers, fancy candles, and other little luxuries to elevate our home.

IT'S BETTER FOR THE PLANET

I'm always looking for ways to reduce my environmental footprint. A smaller home uses less energy and resources and produces far less waste than a larger home. Heating and utility bills are smaller because there's less space to heat and cool. Cleaning products can be reduced because there's less to clean (we use a single all-purpose cleaner for our entire home!). A smaller home requires space dwellers to consume less, which also means less packaging and less waste.

QUALITY OF LIFE

I am restless by nature and love traveling, eating out, going to meet friends, and having city adventures and day trips. I love spending time with my family at home, but it can sometimes start to feel a little too cozy. The good news is that a smaller home can be a catalyst to connect with friends and neighbors, be more creative and resourceful, and get better acquainted with the world outside of your four walls.

Sure, sharing one tiny bathroom is no picnic, and occasionally I daydream about having a spacious mudroom, but we love our home. Overall, having a small, minimal home has resulted in more time, money, energy, and freedom for our whole family. File that under win-win.

VINTAGE ECLECTIC IN VANCOUVER

FIONA'S STORY

The only child of academic parents, Fiona was a quiet, sensitive girl who loved spending time at home despite her nomadic childhood. Her mother was a speech pathologist, and her father was a linguist who studied East African languages, so the family moved and traveled often. Fiona hopped from country to country and spent time schooling abroad in Europe and Africa. The family's home base was on Newfoundland, the most easterly point in North America. Snowy and frozen most of the year, the island is full of brightly colored homes and surrounded by a spectacular backdrop of cliffs, waterfalls, and glaciers.

Given her extensive travels, Fiona became a treasure collector but was also inherently very tidy and organized. In an unusual role reversal, her parents did not share her love for order and requested that she refrain from tidying the home. As a result, she kept her room immaculate and was left to dream about organizing other people's spaces.

Fiona was encouraged to follow in her parents' footsteps and pursue a career in academia, but after attending university and earning a language degree, she realized it was not her path and made the brave decision to make a career pivot. With a lifelong passion for art and design, she returned to school to study interior design at the British Columbia Institute of Technology. After completing her degree, she worked for a small design firm on home-staging projects and took on a side project—organizing her boyfriend's home. She discovered that she loved helping others improve their day-to-day lives and find freedom through both organization and design.

When the pandemic hit and things shifted at her firm, she took a risk and launched her own home-organizing business. She started by joining Professional Organizers in Canada (POC) and found support among her peers in Vancouver. Many of her colleagues subcontract one another for bigger projects, so she began helping others in the industry as she worked on cultivating her own client roster. She quickly set her business apart by integrating sustainability, styling, and design into her home-organizing projects. She works one-on-one to help her clients improve their spaces by repurposing what they have, rearranging furniture, and sourcing only what they truly need. Fiona's process is highly personalized and collaborative. She loves to source unique and original pieces from auction houses and estate sales instead of opting for big box stores, and she's also very mindful of the environmental impact of her work. She doesn't throw *anything* in the garbage and takes the time to responsibly donate unwanted items and recycle everything from textiles to metals. Her own eclectic style attracts clients who are collectors and have an appreciation for color, texture, and vintage treasures, making her work less about textbook organization and more about curation and intentionality.

The result? A business that's fueled by her lifelong passion for art, travel, design, and organization and a mission to help others find freedom in their lives and beauty in their homes.

FIONA'S HOME

The first thing I learn about Fiona's home is that it's only three hundred square feet. The cost of living is very high in Vancouver, so she opted to rent a tiny but newly renovated space in a beautiful neighborhood on the beach. The small footprint hasn't stopped her from showcasing her beloved vintage treasures, art, and collectibles that line every wall and surface in sight. Because she owns more treasures from her childhood travels than she has room to display, she plays art curator and frequently swaps out her exhibits, rotating art, objects, and textiles when the spirit moves her. Luckily, a small storage locker on the property is available to store her bike, suitcases, snowboard, skis, school notes, and memorabilia.

Inside the cozy one-room home, Fiona optimizes every possible opportunity for storage: windowsills, cabinet tops, and even the top of her medicine cabinet all serve double duty as shelves for displaying decorative objects and books to maximize the apartment's vertical space. In the kitchen, the only appliance that makes the cut is Fiona's Vitamix (that's right, no toaster or microwave in sight), and she stores pots and pans inside the oven to save cabinet space. She has a single cabinet that serves as her food pantry, and she's fully adopted the ethos of just buying what she needs and shopping only when necessary. As she doesn't have space to host more than a few people, her remaining cabinets house a set of just four plates, bowls, cups, and eating utensils. Utilitarian items like cords and chargers are stored under the bed in shallow bins, and seasonal clothes and accessories are tucked away in storage bags. While she may have minimalist tendencies in some departments, Fiona's extensive collection of vintage clothes, robes, and gowns take up a full wall. Fashion is a focal point of this home. Since the tiny apartment came without a single closet, Fiona has created a makeshift wardrobe out of a hanging rack and a tall metal shelf. Clothing is neatly folded and piled high, while accessories are hidden away in baskets.

With no room for a dining table, Fiona eats on the patio outside when weather allows, but mainly curls up on her cozy velvet couch, often with her tiny cat, Kitty, perched by her side. During our visit, we gathered around her tiny table eating delicious Mediterranean takeout from a nearby restaurant. Since there's little room to host or entertain, Fiona makes the whole city her playground. We enjoyed coffee from a nearby café, homemade ice cream from a local treat shop, and even a beautiful boat ride around the city.

Fiona fully embraces her philosophy: the greatest benefit of living small is the total freedom it provides. "I have the view, and the ocean is my backyard, and I could pack up and move anywhere in an instant," she says with a twinkle in her eye. The world is truly her oyster.

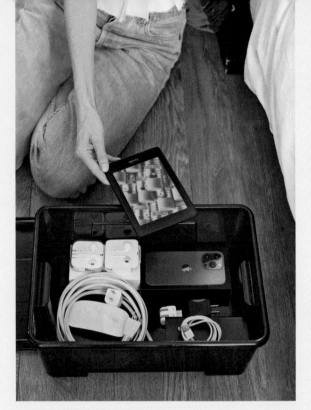

TIPS + TAKEAWAYS

- When you purchase household items (a broom or a hairbrush, for example), take time to select only high-quality items you truly love to use and look at.

- Try a tray: Fiona often uses vintage trays to group and organize her perfume, jewelry, and everyday essentials, as well as her collectibles.

- Use your door for storage and display. Fiona hangs pretty objects on her doorknobs and drapes robes, gowns, or other items from her ever-changing wardrobe rotation.

- Say buh-bye to big box stores. Fiona loves to source from antique dealers and estate sales to find high-quality (and unique) items that will stand the test of time.

- Tuck utilitarian items like cords or batteries in bins or boxes out of sight and use open shelving (even windowsills) to feature your favorite treasures and mementos.

- Store pots and pans inside (or on top of) the oven to maximize space in a tiny kitchen.

- Try the "organized enough" ethos. Fiona doesn't decant her pantry staples into matching, labeled jars. Instead she focuses her energy on grouping similar items together and storing them in intuitive places so she can find what she needs with ease.

- Living small can translate into living large. Soak up the best your city or town has to offer. Be adventurous. Get out and walk, eat, and explore!

Q/A WITH FIONA NURSE

WHAT DO YOU LOVE MOST ABOUT YOUR HOME?
It displays all the pieces that I've collected over the years.

BIGGEST PERSONAL HOME-ORGANIZING CHALLENGE?
Fitting everything into three hundred square feet.

WHAT ARE YOU MOST PROUD OF?
Giving myself creative freedom by starting my own business.

FAVORITE SPACE TO ORGANIZE?
Wardrobes.

DIRTY LITTLE CLUTTER SECRET? ANY AREAS OF YOUR HOME THAT ARE NOT ORGANIZED?
Junk box.

CAN'T-LIVE-WITHOUT ORGANIZING PRODUCT?
Black felt hangers.

MOST TREASURED POSSESSION?
My parents' engagement ring.

GREATEST SPLURGE OR EXTRAVAGANCE?
Travel, vintage clothing, and jewelry.

WHAT'S IN YOUR ORGANIZING TOOLKIT?
Tape measure, notebook, label maker, art hanging kit, hammer, screwdriver, iron, and camera.

MOST COMMON MISCONCEPTION ABOUT PRO ORGANIZERS?
That they are not fun. Haha!

YOUR DEFINITION OF ORGANIZED?
When your space consistently gives you a sense of joy and peace.

BIGGEST TAKEAWAY OR LESSON LEARNED FROM ORGANIZING OTHER PEOPLE'S HOMES?
Material items hold a lot of energy, so getting one's space organized always helps improve mental health and overall well-being.

WHEN YOU'RE NOT ORGANIZING, YOU'RE PROBABLY . . .
Treasure hunting or exploring.

ACTUAL MORNING ROUTINE?
Snuggle with my cat, drink a big glass of water, have vitamins and a smoothie, and do a ten-minute tidy.

ACTUAL EVENING ROUTINE?
Ten minute tidy, skincare routine, relax, and unwind.

ONE SELF-CARE TIP YOU FOLLOW?
Going with my gut feeling, and saying no to things that I don't feel aligned with.

WHAT KIND OF PLANNER DO YOU USE? HOW DO YOU ORGANIZE YOUR DAY?
My iPhone calendar and good old-fashioned notebook.

WHAT MIGHT PEOPLE BE SURPRISED TO LEARN ABOUT YOU?
I'm from the most easterly point in North America, an island off the coast of Canada, but I have lived in different places all over the world.

A RISK YOU TOOK THAT PAID OFF?
Quitting my job to start my own business!

HOW DO YOU RECHARGE WHEN IT'S ALL TOO MUCH?
Spend time with loved ones or do a yoga class.

FAVORITE GIFT TO GIVE?
Jewelry, a unique vintage piece, or anything locally made.

GO-TO DAILY UNIFORM?
Jeans and a T-shirt.

AFRO-CARIBBEAN MEETS WEST COAST COOL

JENNIFER'S STORY

As a sensitive child and empath, Jennifer always craved order, and she used organization to alleviate stress and anxiety from a young age. She always just felt better when her space was neat and aesthetically pleasing. Born and raised in the US Virgin Islands, Jennifer, the oldest of seven siblings, was the go-to person in her family for anything related to planning, organizing, and coordination. She always loved helping others and credits her grandmother (who raised her) for teaching her how to be a superb caregiver. To this day, one of her favorite ways to show love is to wake up super early and cook breakfast for her family before they wake up—a sweet gesture she learned from her grandma.

Guided by a deep yearning to make an impact, Jennifer moved to Miami to study biology and later received a degree in nursing in San Diego. For the next twenty-two years she dedicated her career to the nursing profession caring for patients, but also taking on roles in healthcare administration and teaching. She adored the deep relationships and connections she built in those roles, but after decades of service (plus raising three boys while working full time), Jennifer found herself burned out and exhausted—both mentally and physically drained. She took a leave of absence to rest, regroup, and contemplate her next career move.

Jennifer's gut told her to do something new that related to self-care but launching a product like a candle or bath salts didn't feel meaningful enough. She attended conventions, read books, and brainstormed, writing down lists of all the things she was good at, but nothing clicked. In the meantime, a friend told her about a woman she met who reminded her of Jennifer—and that woman happened to be Tanisha Lyons-Porter, the founder of Natural Born Organizers. She stumbled upon Tanisha a second time while listening to a podcast about how to live a rich, full life. A few months later, their paths crossed a third time when Jennifer, who had been considering becoming a professional organizer, decided to take the leap and join her local chapter of NAPO. With too many signs to ignore, she decided it was time to start her home-organizing business.

Jennifer took classes, hired a business coach, and made a detailed business plan before launching her business with a big home-organizing giveaway. Three years later, she's attracted a loyal fanbase who love her fun,

lighthearted style and kind, empathetic nature. Jennifer's nursing background inspires the methodical process she uses to ensure her clients are fully supported throughout the entire experience, including a comprehensive assessment and seven- and thirty-day post-session check-ins to ensure that the systems she's implemented are effective and maintained.

In addition to continuing to scale her one-on-one organizing business, Jennifer continues to work part-time as a nursing professor, teaching fundamentals and advanced classes. She prides herself on "living an intentional life by design—on her own terms" and finds it deeply satisfying to help others to do the same. She's eager to pass on the lessons she's learned from clearing clutter, creating space, and fostering an intentional and purpose-driven life and career. When speaking about her new profession, Jennifer's whole face lights up. Her entire career has been dedicated to service—however, she's finally created a role for herself that energizes instead of drains her. "I feel a responsibility to serve. I love to serve. And I'm obsessed with my job."

JENNIFER'S HOME

When it comes to decorating her home, Jennifer draws most of her inspiration from her family's Afro-Caribbean roots. She has a collection of African masks dating back twenty years, and she uses them, along with other art, objects, and textiles that feel representative of her family heritage, to decorate her home. Her living spaces are adorned with additional decor from all over the world, highlighting countries she's traveled to or aspires to travel to: a kite and teacups from China, treasures from local African markets, puppets from Indonesia, and an assortment of framed textiles in shadow boxes. Instead of following trends, Jennifer surrounds herself with timeless pieces that feel authentic and heartfelt, and she's always got travel on the brain.

Jennifer discovered her home on an unplanned open house tour, and it was love at first sight. She fell hard for the tall windows and ceilings and the sundrenched entry, and she knew instantly that it was "the one." She's personally designed and furnished each room, including a kitchen renovation where she refaced her cabinets in a rich, dramatic blue and installed new countertops, backsplash, and appliances. The kitchen is beautifully organized without being overly fussy. Jennifer doesn't decant and custom label her spices like many organizers but instead keeps them accessible and tidily displayed on tiered organizers. She has also cleverly repurposed a bank of cabinets into a centralized "appliance closet," where she stores infrequently used appliances as well as party and entertaining supplies, including disposables, platters, and cake stands.

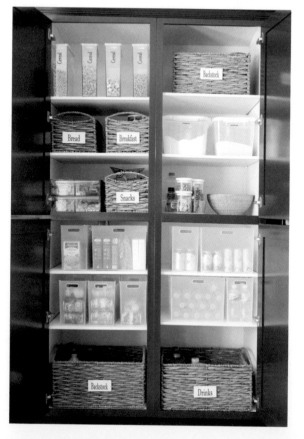

A self-described introvert, Jennifer is still a natural and welcoming host, and her home is designed to make her guests feel comfortable. In the living room, an oversize sectional sofa provides ample seating for family lounging, movies, and snacks. She jokes that it's way too big for the space but loves that it can fit extended family and friends.

Without a dedicated home office, Jennifer has created a stylish work nook below the dramatic staircase across from the dining room. She's used a rug, lamp, and plant to define the space and make it feel like its own little room. With no storage for workspace essentials, she created a simple system: a woven basket on wheels that contains current files, books, and reference materials for easy access. Since the home doesn't have a linen closet, she bundles linens into neatly folded packages and keeps only a few spare sets.

To avoid objects from piling up in the house, Jen and her boys undertake massive cleanouts and donation runs each year before school starts and before Christmas. This consistent effort ensures that the home stays clutter-free and easy to clean and maintain. While Jennifer spends most of her time downstairs in the kitchen, living room, and office nook, her boys are partial to the cozy game room she's created on the landing above the stairs where they play, lounge, and hang out with friends. Every Friday the whole family pitches in to clean and reset the entire house for the weekend, and ongoing maintenance in the house is a team effort. Jennifer's boys have a thorough and detailed weekly chore chart. (Photocopies were made. Get ready, kids!)

Jennifer wants her home to always feel warm and welcoming and for guests to feel like they're at home. Not only has she created a personal, meaningful home, but it's so inviting that you do want to take off your shoes, hop on the couch, and stay awhile. As Jennifer likes to say: "Surround yourself with things that represent the life you want to create."

ORGANIZED LIVING

TIPS + TAKEAWAYS

- Repurpose household items in clever and new ways. Jennifer turned a chip-and-dip stand into a stylish hand- and dish-soap tray.

- Create a home office in a box using a basket on wheels. Stock with files, books, and current reference materials you need to easily access.

- DIY objects into art—Jennifer mounted Balinese finger puppets in a frame with a papyrus background.

- Use small organza bags to store your tiny tech accessories. Tie the bags directly to the equipment so you'll never lose or misplace them again.

- Transform a nook into a home office. Add a rug, lamp, and plant to define the space.

- Try the Friday reset: Dedicate some time to cleaning and tidying each Friday so you can relax and enjoy your weekend.

- Keep clutter at bay with a scheduled seasonal sweep of your living spaces. Jennifer and her family go big on decluttering before birthdays, before school starts, and holidays.

- Give back: If you're having a hard time donating an item, think of a specific family or person who would benefit from having the item.

Q/A WITH JENNIFER DU BOIS

WHAT DO YOU LOVE MOST ABOUT YOUR HOME?
I love all the light that comes in through the windows in our main room.

BIGGEST PERSONAL HOME-ORGANIZING CHALLENGE?
Our tiny linen closet. It has forced me to really pare down to the essentials.

FAVORITE SPACE TO ORGANIZE?
I don't have a space, but I do have a favorite type of project. I see the biggest transformations with whole-home projects.

DIRTY LITTLE CLUTTER SECRET?
My photos! I'm horrible at putting them in albums. All of my children's baby books are half done. Our pictures are in boxes, in no particular order.

CAN'T-LIVE-WITHOUT ORGANIZING PRODUCT?
Baskets! I use them in every room in my home. I love that they are both functional and beautiful.

MOST TREASURED POSSESSION?
A recipe that was handwritten by my grandmother who passed away a few years ago.

FAVORITE ORGANIZING HACK?
Using pouches to organize the contents in my handbag.

BIGGEST TAKEAWAY OR LESSON LEARNED FROM ORGANIZING OTHER PEOPLE'S HOMES?
There is a story behind every behavior and a person behind the clutter, so judgment should never be a part of the equation.

WHEN YOU'RE NOT ORGANIZING, YOU'RE PROBABLY . . .
I love spending time with my family, visiting model homes, and listening to audiobooks.

ACTUAL MORNING ROUTINE?
I start my day by spending time alone. I'll shower and get dressed for the day before I engage with others.

ACTUAL EVENING ROUTINE?
I try my best to complete the most pressing things on my to-do list. Then, I'll watch TV or scroll through social media with my hubbs next to me. We usually end our day sharing a cup of tea together.

THE MOST VALUABLE CAREER ADVICE YOU'VE EVER BEEN GIVEN?
Learn your customer, their likes, desires, pain points. Think of them as a single person, even give them a name so that it feels more personal. Then, commit to speaking to and serving that person and no one else.

A RISK YOU TOOK THAT PAID OFF?
I walked away from a job that broke me mentally. I took some time off to heal and initially planned on returning. However, after months away, I decided not to return. Instead I went full force toward growing my organizing business. It has been the best career decision of my life! I have served the most amazing clients and have been given some great opportunities. I am the happiest I have been in a long time.

HOW DO YOU RECHARGE WHEN IT'S ALL TOO MUCH?
I turn to solitude. Time alone is my favorite self-care activity. In this space, I am able to quiet my mind and ground myself.

WIEBKE LIU

SUSTAINABLE STYLE
BY THE BAY

WIEBKE'S STORY

Life can be full of surprises, and Wiebke's unexpected career journey from the top of the corporate ladder to a niche career setting up stylish and sustainable pantries is no exception. Raised in Düsseldorf, Germany, Wiebke was a dedicated student with a sharp mind for strategic thinking and problem-solving. After high school, she completed a rigorous training and certification program in banking and wealth management at Deutsche Bank, followed by a degree at the University of Washington.

Post-graduation, she landed a coveted business analyst position working at McKinsey & Company (one of the world's most prestigious strategy consulting firms). By this time, she had reunited with her high school sweetheart, Fred, who she had met during her time as a high school exchange student in Saint Louis, Missouri. After her McKinsey years, Wiebke focused on sales and marketing roles. She worked in Silicon Valley start-ups, as well as for giant companies, and even started her own marketing and sales agency. She loved working both in large businesses and small, entrepreneurial settings.

Eventually, Wiebke felt that it was time to leave the fast-paced consulting world and figure out her next move. She was sure she would land in corporate strategy or marketing. Little did she know that her next career move lay in her kitchen remodel. The renovation had required the family to unload and relocate all their pantry staples into laundry baskets in the spare bedroom. When the work was complete, Wiebke was faced with a massive pile of food stored in plastic bags that were held together with chip clips. She couldn't bring herself to shove the mess back into her pristine new cabinets and knew there had to be a better solution. She remembered how, after the war, her grandma had decanted the bulk baking staples she had received from CARE, (the international humanitarian organization that supported families in war-torn Europe) into hermetically sealed glass jars. The donations were a lifeline, and she was not going to waste a single scoop of flour or sugar. Taking a page from her grandma's playbook, she decided to organize her own products into clear glass jars. In a single afternoon, she decanted all her baking supplies, pantry staples, and snacks and was thrilled with the result but horrified by the volume of plastic packaging and waste that lay before her. Another light-bulb moment! Wiebke decided she wanted to make drastic changes to the way she consumed, avoiding plastic as much as possible. She researched her local markets to find the ones that offered staples in bulk and brought her own cloth or paper bags to replenish her jars. Her husband and two kids were on board with the lifestyle shift, with a few minor exceptions, like Fred's favorite potato chips that came in single-use bags and her daughter's string cheese, which was wrapped in plastic. As a result, Wiebke invented the clever and cheeky "hall pass," a get-out-of-jail card for plastic use so each family member could still enjoy a few of their favorite treats, guilt-free.

Wiebke could easily identify the contents of each jar, but when she realized Fred couldn't distinguish between jars, she decided to design her own custom labels complete with baking instructions and cook times! When friends and family saw her pantry reveal, they gasped, prompting Fred to suggest she turn her passion project into a business. She piloted the program with friends and family (you're looking at lucky test case number eleven right here!) and dubbed the new venture Blisshaus.

Her major career breakthrough happened when she organized and styled a pantry for designer Jon de la Cruz, who was featuring a kitchen project in the San Francisco Decorator Showcase. The stunning space was selected as the "Kitchen of the Year" for *House Beautiful*, and the exposure gave Wiebke all the credibility she needed to book other high-end projects for families, individuals, influencers, and celebrities. Her dream pantry make-overs garnered attention from the press, including features in *Goop*, *House Beautiful*, *Lonny*, and *Remodelista*. As demand grew for her "pantry with a purpose," she launched DIY Blisshaus kits, complete with recipe cards, a starter set of labeled jars, a funnel for decanting, and cloth bags perfectly sized for plastic-free bulk-bin shopping. She dove into scaling her business, training full-service teams in Los Angeles, South Carolina, Dallas, and even in London, where the family recently relocated for two years. In addition to full-service pantry makeovers, Wiebke designed systems for plastic-free laundry rooms (powdered detergent, clothes pins, and wool dryer balls in labeled glass jars), junk drawers, and even pet stations.

Her business and growing brand has inspired clients all over the world to reduce their consumption of plastic and processed foods and to cook more, eat better, and enjoy their time in the kitchen.

Wiebke is working on a book and a video and workshop series that will include her signature process coupled with fresh, seasonal recipes. Her joyful nature and passion for hosting and entertaining informs all her work, as evidenced by her brand tagline: "Style and sustainability made simple."

WIEBKE'S HOME

Unsurprisingly, Wiebke's sunny kitchen is the heart of her home, and the place where everyone tends to gravitate and gather. Every time I've had the pleasure of visiting, I've been greeted with warm Bundt cakes, chewy cookies, or candied nuts and sugar-coated cranberries served in martini glasses. Twist my arm!

Cooking has always been Wiebke's number one creative outlet and stress reliever, and it feels like her entire home is built around cooking and entertaining with ease. The cheery dining room is well-stocked with liquor, flowers, fruit, and treats and opens up to a spacious and sunny patio where the family loves to host and entertain.

The family shops for fresh staples, produce, and flowers at the weekly farmers' market, and the haul (including farm-fresh eggs kept at room temperature), is displayed in large bowls on the kitchen counter for easy cooking and snacking access.

The large fridge is filled with the provisions the family enjoys—cheeses, charcuterie, sparkling beverages, and homemade treats. Fresh veggies like kale, carrots, and asparagus, as well as herbs, are propped up in little glasses with water to keep them fresh. One of Wiebke's favorite hacks is to store all her food storage containers in the fridge *even* when they are clean and empty. This trick makes it easy to load up leftovers after mealtime and frees up space in kitchen cabinets and drawers. Wiebke even takes the empty containers to the butcher and fishmonger to transfer meat and fish directly into the containers. That's dedication!

In the lower cabinets, pull-out wooden drawers reveal the impressive collection of Blisshaus jars and brightly printed labels, which contain an array of baking staples, dry goods, and snacks. A single drawer has been outfitted with Wiebke's extensive spice collection, all decanted into sleek jars with her self-designed labels. The food wraps and knickknack drawer are especially charming, with labeled jars containing birthday candles, confetti, and even "thingy mabobs."

To reduce waste, Wiebke's compost bin is mounted under the sink and is dumped, rinsed, and put in the dishwasher after use—no liners or bags necessary. Elsewhere in the kitchen, daily-use dishes are stacked up in low drawers by the dishwasher so kids can unload and set the table with ease.

Wiebke loves to celebrate all holidays, frying up potato pancakes for Hannukah, dumplings on the Lunar New Year, baking hamantaschen for Purim, and even making green eggs on Saint Patrick's Day. She believes that every day should be a celebration, and she uses the good china and silver daily for family breakfast and even the most casual of mealtimes. Treats and snacks are served on trays or in little dishes or cocktail glasses, so every afternoon feels like a party. You better believe that I ran out to buy a small tray and martini glasses to elevate my own social snacking after we met. Wiebke encourages creativity in the kitchen, and her girls love to bake and experiment. Colorful jars filled with chocolates, sprinkles, s'mores kits, and confetti make this kitchen a child's dream laboratory.

One of Wiebke's fondest childhood memories is of her godmother's traditional Sunday night family feasts. She would shop at the farmers' market, cook all day, and always include an extra place setting for whoever stopped by so they would feel instantly welcomed. Wiebke has clearly followed in her footsteps—her home is always stocked with tea, jam, champagne, treats, and cake stands just waiting for the next gathering or soiree. When I ask what she does when she's not working, Wiebke exclaims with a wink, "We bake, we eat, we celebrate!" Her grandma would be proud.

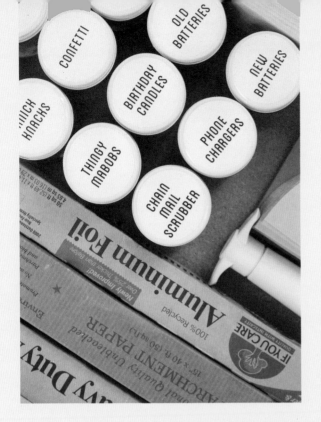

TIPS + TAKEAWAYS

- Store your herbs, carrots, celery, and kale in glasses filled with water in the fridge door. Wiebke calls them her "fridge vases."

- Set up your food storage containers in your fridge (even when clean and empty!) to save space and make it easy to store leftovers and meal prep.

- Save space in your fridge by buying farm-fresh eggs at the farmers' market. They will stay fresh at room temperature on your counter for weeks.

- Use adjustable wooden drawer dividers, and line drawers with cork to eliminate slippage in your flatware and utensil drawers.

- Repurpose household containers whenever possible. Wiebke uses French yogurt cups to store art supplies, glass milk bottles to store beverages and broth, and vases to store herbs and vegetables.

- Make every day a celebration. Use the good china, enjoy the nice silver, and serve snacks and treats in martini glasses.

Q/A WITH WIEBKE LIU

BIGGEST PERSONAL HOME-ORGANIZING CHALLENGE?
My cookbooks. I might need an intervention!

FAVORITE SPACE TO ORGANIZE?
Kitchens because it's where most of the nurturing, cooking, and bonding happens for families. It's the scents and flavors that anchor you to the warmth and love of your inner circle and the place where you explore new tastes and cultures.

DIRTY LITTLE CLUTTER SECRET? ANY AREAS OF YOUR HOME THAT ARE NOT ORGANIZED?
My linen closet keeps falling victim to my cookbook collection.

MOST TREASURED POSSESSION?
My grandfather's paintings and my children's art. And, of course, Juno—our big, fluffy Bernese mountain dog.

GREATEST SPLURGE OR EXTRAVAGANCE?
For the home, I love candlelight and I splurge on fancy candles. My current favorites are Santal by Diptyque and St. John's Wood by Tatine. Also, buying all organic food at our cooperatives is an extravagance and such a privilege. As a family, we treat ourselves by eating out at great restaurants with our kids and taking trips back to Europe.

WHAT DO YOU DO WHEN YOU FEEL OVERWHELMED IN A HOME OR SPACE?
We've literally had team members hyperventilate in the chaos that ensues once you start sorting a kitchen! It's important to remember that things get worse before they get better. When I feel overwhelmed in a home, I remind myself of our three Blisshaus Ds: Deep clean, Decant, Design.

MOST COMMON MISCONCEPTION ABOUT PRO ORGANIZERS?
Some folks think pro organizers have their entire life neatly sorted. Far from it. While I love puzzling out our clients' kitchens and setting up a self-maintaining pantry, my email inbox is packed to the brim, the past four out of five years we sent our Christmas cards around Easter, and I've missed more flights than I can count!

YOUR DEFINITION OF ORGANIZED?
A space is organized when a stranger can come into the home, find what they are looking for, and it's simple for them to return the item. Our team calls this the Airbnb test: could an Airbnb guest find the item and see where it belongs?

BIGGEST TAKEAWAY OR LESSON LEARNED FROM ORGANIZING OTHER PEOPLE'S HOMES?
Kitchen shame is real. Folks are embarrassed about the mess on their shelves and in their drawers. They think they are the only ones with jumbled boxes and overflowing baggies.

ACTUAL MORNING ROUTINE?
Every morning we sit down to our breakfast of toast with orange marmalade, coffee, and soft-boiled eggs, a tradition from my German childhood. It's a lovely anchor for the family to start the day together. Also, I do set the breakfast plates, knives, spoons, and egg cups on the table the night before.

ACTUAL EVENING ROUTINE?
Starting the dishwasher, pouring a glass of wine (or cup of tea, if I'm good), and plopping on the couch to snuggle with our big Bernese.

THE MOST VALUABLE CAREER ADVICE YOU'VE EVER BEEN GIVEN?
At McKinsey, we analyzed massive amounts of data, and again and again the Pareto principle emerged from the facts: 20 percent or less of the effort generated 80 percent or more of the results—amazing! Cull your activities to focus on the top 20 percent that give you all that bang.

DAILY UNIFORM
Black everything with silver slides.

THE SANCTUARY

MARGARIDA'S STORY

Margarida learned at an early age how to create order and peace from the outside in. Born in Santarém, Portugal, she was a deeply sensitive child who taught herself to calm her anxiety through organization. She loved creating elaborate homes and neighborhoods for her dolls to play in, found solace in putting her room in order, and dreamed of spending her days with animals.

As an adult, her career path was varied and stimulating. She became a marine biologist (teaching and going on whale-watching expeditions), worked for the government in the nature conservation department, and became a yoga instructor and certified doula. She was always interested in personal development and service work, and in her free time practiced yoga and meditation and volunteered to lead classes at her local women's prison. While her career was satisfying, it would ultimately be a series of challenging events that would connect her to the most fulfilling work of her life.

After getting married, having a daughter, and designing her dream home on top of a mountain, a painful divorce left Margarida feeling shattered. She had to leave the home she'd lovingly designed and built and moved into a tiny apartment to create a new life with her two-year-old daughter. Doing her best to heal and mend her broken spirits, she tried all of her typical tools (yoga, meditation, journaling), but nothing seemed to work. Desperate to take action that would help her feel better, she began to methodically and systematically declutter her belongings. She touched each item and allowed herself to feel the emotion it evoked and decided with intention what she wanted to keep. Relief followed. She gained confidence. Her spirits lifted a bit. She started feeling more control over her life. Setting up her new home with intention created a cascade of positive changes.

Once Margarida had transformed her home, she wanted to share her knowledge and experience with other women. She volunteered to help her friends apply the same process she used for herself in their homes so she could build a portfolio. A little research connected her to one of the only professional organizers in Portugal, whom she was able to train with in Lisbon. Soon after, she created a simple logo and website, joined a local business networking group, and started booking her first local clients. It was a natural and easy fit. A thoughtful and intuitive guide, Margarida's work extends far beyond organization. She teaches clients how to use their homes as a holistic tool for self-development and knowledge, just as she did with her own home.

Her individual sessions with clients have proved to be so successful and transformative that she's now launched a series of online group programs and workshops so she can share her process with a wider audience.

After transforming her own heartache into personal growth and healing, Margarida has made a career out of sharing her gifts with others, dubbing herself "the home doula." Sometimes great pain can also lead to immense growth, renewal, innovation, and creativity. She now spends her days providing emotional support and guidance to help her clients transform their lives—both from the outside in and the inside out.

MARGARIDA'S HOME

Torres Novas is a tiny town in Portugal known for handmade towels, dried fruits, and a beautiful medieval castle. Margarida greets us with a warm smile, a tray of hot tea and homemade local pastries, and asks, "Do you want to come meet my home?" After snacking on her sunny tiled patio lined with fruit trees, we are treated to a tour. As I walk around inquiring about her space and her belongings, it strikes me that every single item has a story. There's the Spanish rocking horse (with real horsehair!) from the 1920s, found in the basement of her old house, her grandmother's teacup, a framed hand-made pillowcase, and a special plate from Cuba she loves to display. "My house is a collection of all my houses. There's a lot of history here."

Margarida enjoys DIY projects and has personally created much of the decor that accents her home. She's added tassels to hot mitts to make dream catchers (who thinks of this?!), framed a single sage leaf that a friend brought over to clear the home, and she's painted the vintage chairs in the kitchen and made the seat cushions herself. She also painted an archway in her kitchen to define the space and add visual interest.

When it comes to home organization, she prefers to repurpose rather than to buy new products. Cardboard boxes, baskets, wine bottle boxes, strawberry baskets, shoe boxes, and paper bags folded down to create bins all make functional storage vessels. In the entryway, a functional landing station is created from simple shaker pegs and a slim IKEA shoe storage system.

Since a single room contains Margarida's home office, library, and living room, she maintains a very comfortable and minimal space. A small cabinet stores all her paperwork, books are neatly arranged by color, and the room is accented with potted plants and art painted by dear friends. Given the amount of time she spends online, Margarida suspended a plant from a bracket and color-blocked three soothing paint colors on her back wall to create a pleasing and inspiring background for calls and client sessions.

With no storage closets, attic, basement, or garage, a tall armoire (she added shelves) serves as a makeshift linen closet in the laundry room. The small space stores household essentials, like pet supplies, sheets and towels, camping gear, sleeping bags, and seasonal clothes. Suitcases are nested together to maximize space and a single box holds all holiday decor, which mainly consists of festive pillow covers and blankets—no plastic trinkets to be found here!

When helping her eight-year-old daughter, Isabella, set up her room, Margarida wanted to encourage creativity and self-expression while also implementing the fundamentals of organization. Not an easy feat to pull off! Treasures such as a hand-drawn family portrait, peacock feathers, rocks, crystals, art, and figurines are proudly displayed, while simple bins and boxes corral and contain school materials, painting supplies, play food, and toys. Clothes are housed in a single wardrobe, at arm's reach, so Isabella can get dressed and clean up independently. The bed has a concealed trundle for sleepovers and a drawer for toys and bedding below.

While Margarida describes her home as modest, she considers each room to be sacred, "like rooms in a temple." Her bedroom is particularly sparse and calming, containing only a bed, a tiny dresser, and a wardrobe. The white color palette makes it a quiet and peaceful escape for rest and daily meditation. Margarida takes pride in her home and has steadily worked to make it feel like a retreat and an authentic extension and expression of herself. She believes that anyone can achieve a space that feels good, regardless of size or budget: "Having an organized home is not just for wealthy people. It's not just for people with huge homes. It's for everyone. Everyone can have this."

TIPS + TAKEAWAYS

- Frame keepsakes, cards, or even fabric to create your own personalized art. Margarida has framed sketches, leaves, and even an heirloom pillowcase to create her own decor.

- Color-block your home. It's a fun and budget-friendly way to add personality and visual interest to your space. Use painter's tape to separate and define each color.

- Customize your rental by adding contact paper on cabinet faces or painting or swapping out hardware.

- Transform large pieces of cardboard into oversize folders to store kid art during the year. At the end of the school year, have your kids choose a few favorites to keep or photograph and recycle the rest so you can start fresh for the new year.

- Repurpose storage vessels you already own, like berry baskets, mason jars, or even sturdy cardboard boxes.

- Create at least one room in your home that feels like a sanctuary. Margarida uses white linens and curtains to make her bedroom feel like a peaceful retreat.

Q/A WITH MARGARIDA MADEIRA

BIGGEST HOME-ORGANIZING CHALLENGE?
My eight-year-old daughter's room. We're very different—she's a collector and has many childhood treasures, and it's a learning experience to find a middle path to meet both our needs to live harmoniously. Challenging, yes, but deeply impactful in building a healthy, respectful relationship.

WHAT ARE YOU MOST PROUD OF?
Recovering from a traumatic life situation that left me alone with my two-year-old daughter and rebuilding my inner and external homes. I am proud to have transformed my pains into my gifts, creating a new home and serving others as Doula das Casas (Home Doula).

FAVORITE SPACE TO ORGANIZE?
Kitchens and primary bedrooms. Kitchens are the energetic center of the home, so by tackling them, we prepare the entire house for transformation. And the primary bedroom (our seventh chakra and connection to the Divine) is where we retreat, honestly express ourselves, and recharge.

DIRTY LITTLE CLUTTER SECRET?
Our multifunctional room that houses my laundry, firewood in winter, household clothes closet, DIY storage, recycling center, and general household stuff. Without a garage, basement, or loft, this small room can easily turn into chaos!

CAN'T-LIVE-WITHOUT ORGANIZING PRODUCTS?
I love to use baskets. My great-grandfather, Salvador, a craftsman from Algarve in southern Portugal, made the most beautiful baskets, so it's in my genes. I love to use my own handmade felt baskets for drawers and closets and VARIERA boxes from IKEA in kitchens, fridges, and bathrooms!

MOST COMMON MISCONCEPTION ABOUT PRO ORGANIZERS?
That we all suffer from some obsessive-compulsive disorder and live in a "magazine" home!

MOST TREASURED POSSESSION?
Oh, so many treasures! The ceramic soul bird I crafted; a watercolor by Portuguese artist Graça Paz that reminds me of the blue sea of the Algarve, the land of my maternal lineage; an illustration of a pregnant woman by Italian illustrator Cinzia Ghiglian gifted to me while I was pregnant but didn't know; a watercolor by Ana Silvia Agostinho, a Portuguese illustrator and a solo mother like me, representing our family nucleus—me, Isabella, and our cat Jasmim sitting in a hammock supported by two beautiful olive trees.

FAVORITE ORGANIZING TIP OR IDEA?
Declutter first and organize second! Declutter consciously and consider the mantras: "Breathe in, breathe out, and simplify" and "This too shall pass," especially in moments that feel chaotic.

WHAT DO YOU DO WHEN YOU FEEL OVERWHELMED IN A HOME OR SPACE?
I take a pause. I turn inward and create space and silence to receive information and guidance to help me through that moment. And then I restart. Before entering a home, I always create an intention of observation, asking for guidance to serve my client in the most authentic possible way.

BIGGEST TAKEAWAY OR LESSON LEARNED FROM ORGANIZING OTHER PEOPLE'S HOMES?
Organizing truly has a transformational impact on a person's heart, soul, and life. I witnessed this profoundly when I ran into a client a few months after we worked together, and she happily hugged me and exclaimed, "My life has changed!" She had returned to finish her school degree, started swimming again, and took her life back into her hands. This work empowered her.

BEST ADVICE FOR ASPIRING ENTREPRENEURS?
Adjust your boat sails as many times as necessary. A boat never sails in a straight line.

THE FAMILY HOMESTEAD

BRANDIE AND RYAN'S STORY

Raised in a conservative, faith-driven community in Fort Worth, Texas, sisters Brandie and Ryan grew up surrounded by strong Southern women with a ferocious work ethic. The story of their business success is closely connected to their entrepreneurial family, their close-knit community, and their Christian faith. Their mom paved the way, founding her own business when the girls were teenagers. Their older sister, Shannon, followed in her footsteps by launching her own full-service design studio and ten-thousand-square-foot retail outlet, the Feathered Nest.

Brandie took on odd jobs as early as twelve years old and started working for her mother as soon as she finished high school. She was engaged at eighteen, married at nineteen, and started having kids right away (she now has four children), so working in the family business was a great way to maximize her time at home while bringing in her own income. Ryan, who got married and had two children after studying communications and receiving a business degree, also loved the freedom and flexibility of working from home while raising her kids.

While launching a home-organizing business wasn't an instant or obvious choice, it made sense given the sisters' upbringing and natural tendencies. Their father had always set strict standards for the home, including tossing things that weren't properly put away (hear that, kids?), so the girls learned early on how to clean and maintain an organized home. Brandie always had a system and a plan for every aspect of her life, while Ryan loved home styling and design so much that she and her husband personally lived in and flipped *ten* homes, all while raising kids and managing their own careers (she dropped this information casually, like she was ordering a hamburger).

Initially, the idea to start their own business was a way to help pay for their kids' private school tuition. The plan was to take on projects during school hours and work for their mom's business in the evenings after the kids were in bed. Not ones to overthink on an idea, the sisters gave themselves a month to create and launch their professional-organizing company. Ryan taught herself how to build a website from scratch, and Brandie, the "master networker," took the lead on booking their first clients.

The duo immediately went to work testing out new products, creating their own custom labels, and organizing every square inch of their own homes.

They joked that if the business never materialized, at least their homes would look spectacular. Early on, they started showcasing their own projects, featuring candid behind-the-scenes footage on their Instagram platform, which resulted in a loyal fanbase and a growing client roster. They recruited their kids, husbands, and other family members to pitch in on jobs, and as demand grew, the sisters started hiring others from their local community to join the team. Their home-organizing transformations became more and more efficient as the team expanded (they now send anywhere from four to fifteen team members out on a single job), and they've garnered a reputation for meticulously organizing (as well as moving and unpacking) entire homes within a few days.

When it comes to the day-to-day business operations, Brandie oversees all things related to accounting, legal, logistics, and scheduling, while Ryan manages the company website and social media, and pitches new partnerships. The sisters are united by their shared values (both of their husbands work within their church), incredible work ethic, tenacity, and drive. Even when they have a lull between projects or a slower month, they're both actively reaching out to old clients, cultivating new relationships and partnerships, and even cold-calling influencers and celebrities to collaborate.

Among their many achievements, they have hundreds of thousands of loyal Instagram followers, a brand partnership and organizing product line with mDesign, a roster of celebrity clients, and a television series on the Design Network. The sisters also commit a percentage of their yearly income toward supporting a philanthropic organization and cite their proudest business moment as writing a generous check to Agape International Missions, a nonprofit on a mission to support survivors of human trafficking and exploitation.

As a way to foster community within the home-organizing industry, Brandie and Ryan also launched a live professional conference, the HOW TO: Summit. The annual event draws attendees from coast to coast who are eager to connect, network, share resources, and learn from other industry leaders. Summit speakers have included marketing and social media experts, brand strategists, CEOs, attorneys, and a wide panel of top organizers in the field. I've been fortunate to speak at the summit each year, and let me tell you, these women know how to throw a party. In addition to a packed schedule of speakers, experts, and panelists, there are balloon photo walls, taco trucks, prize packages, giveaways, comedy sketches (a satire on how to fold a fitted sheet brought the house down), social mixers, and dance parties.

When I inquire how they manage to create such an incredible event year after year while running a full-time business and raising six kids between them, they credit hard work and their incredible support system. As both sisters tell me multiple times, "Family is everything."

Brandie's and Ryan's homes each have their own flavor and personality, but there are more similarities than differences. Both homes are heavily furnished from their sister's design studio and feature stylish and functional products from their home-organizing line with mDesign.

BRANDIE'S HOME

Brandie's home sits on five acres of land, a space she shares with her family of six, as well as a goat, a pig, six sheep, and two dogs. Maintaining a well-edited home is especially challenging when you have ample space, so everything in Brandie's home feels truly purposeful and intentional. Snacks are stored in clear, labeled bins at arm's reach in the pantry (it didn't take long for me to find the Cheez-Its), and everything from vitamins to charging cords to art supplies are categorized, organized, and clearly labeled for easy grab-and-go access.

The closet Brandie shares with her husband looks like a boutique, complete with clear, labeled shoe boxes and storage baskets for seasonal and occasional items. Since the family doesn't have a home office, she has set up a compact work-from-home station in her bedroom credenza. Behind closed doors, she's arranged tape, pens, pencils, labeling supplies, gift cards, stationery, mementos, and business documents, impeccably organized in clear, acrylic bins and pull-out baskets. Her oversize nightstands reveal more labeled bins, containing seasonal and travel accessories, as well as utility supplies that used to float around the house but now have designated homes of their own. Especially charming is the family's mini library at the end of the hallway, connecting the bedrooms. Since the kids don't have bookshelves in their bedrooms, Brandie has centralized everyone's books into an inviting book station for all to enjoy. The living spaces are elevated with furniture, lighting, and decor from her sister Shannon's design studio, and Brandie explains, "Things that look good just make me happy. I can't be my best self if my house is not in order. It's not about making things look perfect, it's about feeling good."

RYAN'S HOME

Ryan and her husband personally designed and remodeled their charming 1,200-square-foot bungalow situated on a full acre of land. Ryan took the lead on all the design decisions, including tiles, flooring, lights, and finishes, while her husband, Ben, completed all of the manual labor, including tiling, painting, and electrical work. Since the home is tight on space with no attic, basement, or garage, it was essential to pare down and get clever with storage solutions. The two kids store their shoes, jackets, and backpacks in their own closets instead of by the front door and are disciplined about returning homework and school supplies to their rooms. Musical instruments are mounted on the walls of their bedroom, and their music books, sewing supplies, and other hobbies are stored in bins in their own closets.

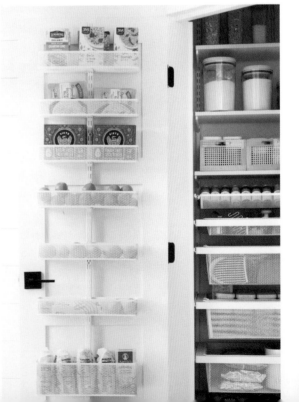

In the bedroom, Ryan has claimed the small closet, and Ben (who luckily dresses casually) stores his entire wardrobe in a single dresser. Ryan added a narrow shelf and single chair to her closet beneath her shoes, creating a mini vanity. Brilliant.

In the kitchen, a total of just three drawers and two small cabinets (the other two cabinets conceal the tiny fridge and garbage cans) house the pots and pans, strainer, mixing bowls, flatware, and an electric mixer.

A slim wall shelf mounted above the range displays cutting boards, cooking utensils, serving bowls, and a set of modern white ceramic dinnerware, with the overflow stacked neatly on the counter. Most everything in the kitchen is carefully curated for cohesiveness and aesthetics and stored at arm's reach. In the adjacent dining room, an upholstered bench doubles as storage for extra serving pieces, large platters, china, and occasional-use appliances. A slim pantry? No problem! Their pantry is optimized with floor-to-ceiling shelves, pull-out drawers, and additional storage bins mounted to the inside of the door. Ingeniously, it also houses the microwave, toaster, and a handful of small appliances, as well as glassware, spices, canned goods, sauces, cooking and baking staples, and even fresh fruit. In the rest of the home, Ryan uses concealed storage to tuck away utilitarian essentials. In their bedroom, a decorative trunk at the foot of the bed houses blankets and sheets. In the entry, cleaning products are organized out of sight in a storage bench, and a small safe contains important documents, memorabilia, taxes, and external hard drives. Ben built a workshop in the backyard to store his extensive collection of tools, and Ryan stores Christmas decor and seasonal clothes in a small off-site storage unit. With no room to store extra products or backstock, Ryan never buys in bulk and chooses to purchase only what she needs when she needs it.

It's remarkable that despite their grueling work schedules, two husbands, six kids, and a fleet of animals between them, Brandie and Ryan have found it easy to maintain tidy, stylish, and organized homes. The sisters credit simple systems, as well as involving the whole family. They've taught their children the life skills of being tidy and respectful of their belongings. In both homes, everyone in the family contributes and works as a collective to clean, tidy, and maintain order, taking turns with the dishes, taking out trash, feeding the animals, and even touching up paint and helping with home repairs and maintenance. Taking pride in your home is an important value and one that the sisters are proud to pass on to their kids. As Brandie quips, " 'My kids are slobs, and I love it,' said no one ever."

TIPS + TAKEAWAYS

- Conceal the cords! Ryan has mounted charging cords on the wall side of each bed, adhering mini power strips with Command hooks. She also recommends feeding cords through drawers or tucking them neatly behind furniture.

- Involve the whole family in daily cleaning and chores, instilling the value that shared space is a shared responsibility.

- Repurpose stylish furniture to suit your storage needs. Ryan uses her dining room bench for platters and appliances, while Brandie stores household essentials and office supplies in her bedroom credenza and nightstands.

- Create a simple vanity in your small closet just by adding a single shelf and chair or stool.

- Use handled bins to create your own pull-out "drawers" wherever you need them.

- Reality check: Be realistic about the space you have, NOT the space you wish you had! "Stop shopping for a mansion when you live in a cottage."

Q/A WITH BRANDIE LARSEN

WHAT WAS YOUR BIGGEST PERSONAL HOME-ORGANIZING CHALLENGE?
We have a big family and minimal storage.

DIRTY LITTLE CLUTTER SECRET?
YES! We have a spare room that has become the place everything gets temporarily tossed. Some days, you can't even walk in the room!

WHAT IS YOUR MOST TREASURED POSSESSION?
My family. Everything else is replaceable.

WHAT MIGHT PEOPLE BE SURPRISED TO LEARN ABOUT YOU?
I am really hard on myself, and I usually expect myself to have it all together.

GO-TO DAILY UNIFORM?
Something stretchy and comfortable. Then add a designer sneaker to keep myself from looking like I rolled out of bed!

BIGGEST LESSON OR TAKEAWAY FROM ORGANIZING OTHER PEOPLE'S HOMES?
Too many people are living with too much stuff, and then they're frustrated. Live in the space you have, not the space you wish you had!

A RISK YOU TOOK THAT PAID OFF?
Pitching big ideas and leading with the attitude "all they can do is say no!"

MOST COMMON MISCONCEPTION ABOUT PRO ORGANIZERS?
That we are all type A, spreadsheet-keeping people. I love to be in charge, but that is where the type A ends for me!

THE MOST VALUABLE CAREER ADVICE YOU'VE EVER BEEN GIVEN?
You can have it all, but not always at the same time.

Q/A WITH RYAN EIESLAND

WHAT WAS YOUR BIGGEST PERSONAL HOME-ORGANIZING CHALLENGE?
Having enough storage while also having a small home.

DIRTY LITTLE CLUTTER SECRET?
My husband's work shed is a disaster, and he won't let me organize it.

THE MOST VALUABLE CAREER ADVICE YOU'VE EVER BEEN GIVEN?
You may not be the smartest in the room, but you can always be the hardest worker.

FAVORITE GIFT TO GIVE?
I love giving luxury hotel stays to my family, and Jeni's ice-cream delivery is my go-to for friends.

BIGGEST TAKEAWAY OR LESSON LEARNED FROM ORGANIZING OTHER PEOPLE'S HOMES?
Consumerism is a serious problem.

WHAT IS YOUR MOST TREASURED POSSESSION?
My family photos and videos.

WHAT DO YOU DO WHEN YOU FEEL OVERWHELMED IN A HOME OR SPACE?
Clean.

MOST COMMON MISCONCEPTION ABOUT PRO ORGANIZERS?
We are all minimalists.

ONE SELF-CARE TIP YOU FOLLOW?
Saying no when I need to. Saying yes when I need to.

There is no doubt about it, between birthday parties, homework, activities, and hobbies, living with kids means managing a whole lot of stuff. Read on for tips on how to keep the clutter at bay and your sanity intact.

LIMIT THE VOLUME

While there is so much pressure to consume all the latest trendy toys, an overstuffed playroom can be overstimulating, distracting, and stressful for kids and parents alike. Instead, invest in a handful of timeless and versatile items, like building blocks, boardgames, books, and art supplies. Remember: The less stuff you own, the less you (and your kiddos) have to manage and clean up.

KEEP IT SIMPLE

When it comes to toy organization, simple is always best. Open floor bins or baskets are ideal for storing blocks, balls, stuffed animals, play food, and dress-up. Pouches or toolboxes can contain tiny toys and delicate collections. Board games and puzzles can be lined up on a shelf or unboxed and stored in individual baskets or oversize zip pouches. A single rolling cart can contain art supplies, science kits, and specialty projects. Keeping your systems simple and accessible will help empower kids to clean up independently.

ZONES, SWEET ZONES

Set your home up like a kindergarten classroom by grouping all items into big, broad intuitive categories. Zoning your child's toys, books, and games will provide a visual cue of what goes where and make cleanup a breeze. Many organizing pros opt to store all of their kids' playthings and belongings in their respective rooms or closets so kids can manage their own things and keep their clutter out of shared living spaces.

MAINTENANCE MODE

No need to sing the clean-up song, but a five-minute tidy can go a long way toward keeping your home feeling good. Transition times, like before dinner or bedtime, are a great time to remind your kids to put away toys, projects, homework, and clothes and reset their space for the next day.

LET'S GET DIGITAL

You'd be hard pressed to find an organizer who has a basement crammed with bins of kid art and mementos. Instead, most opt to keep a handful of treasures and digitize the rest. A single binder with clear sleeves can be used to store the most precious school photos, certificates, and awards.

TRY A "LENDING LIBRARY"

Reduce the visible volume of toys and games in your home and store the rest in a "lending library," so you can rotate toys out as interests change and evolve. You can also include friends and neighbors in the rotation, so you can swap with each other instead of buying new things.

SHARED SPACE MEANS SHARED RESPONSIBILITY

Divvy up the chores in a way that feels both equitable and age appropriate. Empower your children to help with cooking, dishes, laundry, cleaning, and even painting or household repairs. Even very young kids can help with small tasks like matching their socks, bringing in mail, or sweeping. Their involvement may make them feel differently about how they treat the space.

CENTRALIZE THE TREASURES

What you consider trash may be your child's most valued treasure. I beg my kids not to bring home plastic party favors (and I encourage you not to distribute them), but it's inevitable that you'll find plastic gizmos, collectibles, or pet rocks floating around your home. Set up a designated "treasure bin" for each of your children, so your kids can curate and manage current favorites themselves. The only rule? Parents can't touch what's in the bin. When the bin reaches capacity, it's up to your kids to edit it to create space for incoming treasures.

MAKE AN OUT-THE-DOOR CHECKLIST

Tired of reminding your kids to brush their teeth or pack up lunches before they scoot out the door? Make an out-the-door checklist to post near the front door for easy reference. Common reminders include making the bed, clearing breakfast dishes, feeding the pets, brushing teeth, applying sunscreen, and packing up homework, sports gear, water bottles, snacks, and lunches. This will lead to less nagging, items left behind, and stress each morning.

TRY A WEEKLY FAMILY MEETING

A weekly check-in meeting (I suggest Sundays) can provide a great opportunity to connect with your people, review upcoming events and logistics, and plan the week ahead. A sample agenda might include appreciation and compliments,

calendar and logistics review, meal planning, and restocking lists for food and household supplies. Add snacks, games, music, or anything else to personalize your meeting. When we take the time to gather and get on the same page as a family, I notice a profound difference in the flow and ease of our days and weeks ahead.

LIVEABLE LUXURY
IN ATLANTA

BRITTANI'S STORY

Unlike many of the people featured in this book, organization was always a major struggle for Brittani, even into adulthood. Born in Wichita, Kansas, and raised in Atlanta, Georgia, by her mom, Brittani was a self-described tomboy who loved playing outside. She was a straight-A and civically active student, but while she was consistently a high performer in school, keeping her room tidy did not come naturally. Brittani laughs recalling that her friends would offer to help her clean her room so she could go hang out with them.

Brittani attended the honors program at Spelman College, where she met and married her husband, Chris, who was studying business at Morehouse College nearby. Chris started a corporate career straight out of school, while Brittani graduated with a degree in biology and decided to pursue a master's degree in biomedical science. The couple started a family right away, and after contemplating medical school, Brittani realized that becoming a doctor wasn't compatible with the vision she had for her life, especially as a new mother (she now has two kids).

Once she completed her master's degree, she was bit by the entrepreneurial bug and launched a small consulting business helping high school upperclassman plan their college direction. After spending more than a year focused on strategic academic planning with parents and teens, she closed the business to contemplate her next move.

Suddenly home all the time, juggling kids and carpools and domestic responsibilities, Brittani felt overwhelmed by the influx of laundry and dishes. She was always misplacing important documents and felt sheer panic when friends or family came over. It was a shove-everything-in-the-closet situation. As hard as she tried, she just couldn't seem to keep up, and after dropping her kids off at school, her entire day turned into an endless cycle of cooking, laundry, cleaning, and tidying. Although she did pick up blogging, using her human biology background to share expert advice on how to create a healthy, nontoxic home, this feeling of overwhelm hindered her ability to plan her next career move.

It was a vacation stay at a minimalist Airbnb rental that made her realize how light and free she felt with less stuff to manage. She picked up a copy of Marie Kondo's book, *The Life-Changing Magic of Tidying Up*. The book detailed a methodical process for decluttering the entire home, one category at a time. Brittani realized that organization could be a learned skill, and for the first time she felt hopeful that she could actually acquire it. She finished the book within days and decided to follow the process to systematically work through every square inch of her home. Brittani took the project on as a full-time job, donating furniture, decor, and housewares and organizing and styling the items she kept with care. Within a month she had transformed her home and her life.

With less stuff to manage and an organized home, her time and energy were freed up to focus on her life and career. She enrolled in a business course and launched a product guide for creating a healthy, nontoxic home. Brittani took the process that had worked so well for her and started helping friends and family members declutter and organize their homes. She changed her blog and business name from Pinch of Health to Pinch of Help and shared her transformations on Instagram, attracting new clients inspired by her dramatic home makeovers. Chris was climbing the corporate banking ladder, but as Brittani's organizing business started gaining traction, they decided to team up and go all in on growing her business together. The decision for Chris to walk away from a successful and lucrative corporate career was motivated by the desire to spend more time together as a family.

Although there were bumps in the road, the couple quickly sorted out how to divide and conquer, recognizing and honoring their individual strengths and weaknesses. Brittani remained at the helm as the visionary and creative but pivoted from hands-on organizing to overseeing sales, marketing, social media, and partnerships. Chris now serves as the lead on all projects and has also used his business background to implement structure and systems to oversee hiring and team growth.

Brittani, who once had deep shame about the state of her home, now uses her skillset to help entrepreneurs, athletes, and other busy professionals overhaul their homes and simplify their lives. She empathizes deeply with her clients' challenges, recalling that she used to think that clutter and disorganization would be a forever struggle. Her personal breakthrough has not only impacted her own life but serves as inspiration and motivation for her loyal client base. Brittani's work and process have helped inspire thousands of people, and she is thrilled to be able to make such a positive impact on others who are struggling: "When something changes your life, you want to share it."

BRITTANI'S HOME

Walking into Brittani's open and airy family home, you would never guess that she once struggled with clutter and disorganization. Her living spaces are so minimal and tidy that I inquire if her teenage kids still lived at home (they do!).

The secret is that they have pared back their home to the essentials—just the things they use, need, and love. In addition to organizing, Brittani loves to style her spaces, combining form and function. The walk-in pantry is straight out of a magazine but still fully functional for their busy family. Oversize floor baskets are stocked with paper goods (plastic packaging removed, of course), canned goods are displayed on tiered organizers, and produce is stored in open market baskets for easy access. Baking essentials are decanted into clear, matching canisters; and clear, labeled bins corral bread, breakfast favorites, smoothie essentials, baking mixes, backup spices, and vitamins. Beverages are lined up like a supermarket display, and bars and kid snacks are set up in turntables at arm's reach, so kids can help themselves. The top shelves display Brittani's favorite vases and cake stands, while the kitchen cabinets house all of her glassware, dishware, pots and pans, utensils, and cooking tools, so the counters can remain clutter-free.

The entry looks remarkably minimal for a busy family of four and only contains Brittani's daily-use bags and sneaker collection, which are stored in clear, stackable drawers. She keeps sports gear in the car, and the rest of the family stores their clothes, shoes, and bags in their own closets (a common theme among the organizers I interviewed).

In the bathroom, an over-the-door organizing system displays robes, slippers, and hair products, while washcloths, combs, towels, sheets, backup products, and paper goods are kept in baskets in the small linen closet.

The primary bedroom is inspired by Brittani's love of hotel living. The space is minimally furnished with a huge, comfy bed, a loveseat with cozy throw pillows primed for lounging, and even a nightstand-turned-beverage-and-snack station stocked with fresh fruit, flowers, and light snacks.

In her teenage daughter's room, a wall-mounted workstation with plenty of vertical shelves creates ample storage for homework supplies, notebooks, paper, and mementos. One of Brittani's favorite space-maximizing tips is to install over-the-door organizing racks with clip-on baskets and hooks. She uses these in her kids' rooms and throughout the home to create extra storage for everything from school supplies to first aid, toiletries, and family essentials, such as sunscreen, hand sanitizer, masks, and water bottles. Inspired after I met with her, I purchased one for my daughter's tiny room and tried to install it myself (let's just say it did not go well—I'm icing my forehead as I write this). I recommend hiring a professional for installation unless you are particularly handy.

To keep the house clean and tidy, Brittani has created a detailed chore system for her kids to follow. One takes full ownership over the kitchen duties, including washing and drying dishes, wiping down surfaces, and sweeping and vacuuming the floors, while the other handles washing, hanging, and folding laundry for the whole family. They alternate responsibilities each month, and everyone keeps their belongings in their rooms, so the living spaces stay clear of clutter. "We're a bedroom family," Brittani says. "At the end of a long day, everyone loves to relax in their own rooms."

It's not often that someone becomes the best at the thing they were the worst at, but after years of struggle, Brittani has cracked the code on creating and maintaining a beautifully organized home.

TIPS + TAKEAWAYS

- Use stackable drawers for shoes in the entry. This helps put a boundary on quantity and avoids a shoe mountain by the front door.

- Turn your junk drawer into a spice drawer! Brittani loves to set up a spice station in a drawer instead of on the counter, using matching, labeled jars so everything is visible at a glance.

- Utilize door-mounted organizers to add storage throughout your home. These simple additions can store school supplies, gift wrap, toiletries, pantry staples, and office supplies.

- Set up a wellness station in one designated area of your home. Brittani's includes masks, hand sanitizer, paper goods, and gloves.

- Make an "out the door" station: centralize the items you (or your kids) reach for most when you're running out the door. An over-the-door system can hold lunch money, lip balm, sunscreen, lotion, lunch boxes, and notepads.

Q/A WITH BRITTANI ALLEN

WHAT DO YOU LOVE MOST ABOUT YOUR HOME?
I love my home's abundant natural light and general lack of clutter.

FAVORITE SPACE TO ORGANIZE?
Bathroom.

DIRTY LITTLE CLUTTER SECRET?
My guest room is only presentable when we actually have guests, which is maybe once a quarter. It definitely warrants a DO NOT ENTER sign from time to time.

MOST TREASURED POSSESSION?
My business.

GREATEST SPLURGE OR EXTRAVAGANCE?
My Vitamix (I leave the more extravagant spending for my husband).

WHAT DO YOU DO WHEN YOU FEEL OVERWHELMED IN A HOME OR SPACE?
Call for backup! Having a team or friends to help cuts down on the overwhelm tremendously. Most jobs are not meant for just one person to handle. And if all else fails, turn on some good music.

MOST COMMON MISCONCEPTION ABOUT PRO ORGANIZERS?
That we only care about the aesthetics of a space.

YOUR DEFINITION OF ORGANIZED?
Knowing where every single item is in your home within seconds.

BEST ADVICE FOR ASPIRING ENTREPRENEURS?
Enjoy all aspects of the journey! Don't wait until you achieve any specific level of success. It will be hard, it will be draining, it will call you to stretch yourself and your abilities in ways you can't imagine, but it will also be beautiful, so enjoy it!

BIGGEST TAKEAWAY OR LESSON LEARNED FROM ORGANIZING OTHER PEOPLE'S HOMES?
That putting organized systems in place can truly change people's lives and relationships. Having a cluttered, disorganized home is stressful in so many ways. Relieving our clients of that stress immediately increases their quality of life, and that is truly priceless.

WHEN YOU'RE NOT ORGANIZING, YOU'RE PROBABLY . . .
Playing tennis or arranging flowers to place around my home. Or watching Netflix. Ha!

ACTUAL MORNING ROUTINE?
First thing in the morning, I drink a tall jug of water with fresh lemon. Then I have devotional time and go over my schedule and to-do list for the day.

ACTUAL EVENING ROUTINE?
I don't have a fancy evening routine. Just a nice hot shower, skin, and oral care, then slipping on some pajamas to watch TV in bed with my husband.

ONE SELF-CARE TIP YOU FOLLOW?
I aim to be in the bed (but not asleep) by 8 p.m. every day. After years of working past 9 p.m., this is a standing appointment I try not to miss . . . unless I'm playing tennis.

THE MOST VALUABLE CAREER ADVICE YOU'VE EVER BEEN GIVEN?
As soon as you start making money, hire a bookkeeper and a CPA. Saves me a ton of stress.

GO-TO DAILY UNIFORM?
My Pinch of Help shirt and black leggings.

WHAT MIGHT PEOPLE BE SURPRISED TO LEARN ABOUT YOU?
That I used to have a terrible time trying to maintain order in my home. And that I didn't intend to start an organizing business. I desperately needed relief from the chaos and clutter, so I decluttered and organized my own home, and that changed my life.

JEN ROBIN

THE BEACH BUNGALOW

JEN'S STORY

Jen Robin has been a high achiever and natural-born problem solver practically since birth. In elementary school she skipped recess to reorganize her class's desks (her own space was already immaculate, and her belongings were color-coded before it was a trend). Leadership came naturally to her, and in addition to being class and student-body president, Jen's life revolved around athletics. She thrived within the rigorous structure and routine inherent with competitive sports and somehow found time to participate in tennis, swimming, basketball, softball, and soccer (and I can barely find time to take a brisk daily walk, but here we are). When her coach urged her to pick one sport to go all-in on, she chose soccer, practicing every free moment she had, morning until night, and eventually landing a full scholarship to a division-one college in Southern California. Like I said—achiever.

A few years after college, she landed a role as the executive assistant for a professional athlete who moved all the time. Jen turned her competitive focus to improving and optimizing every single aspect of her boss's life, taking on the roles of house manager, moving and logistics manager, scheduling coordinator, and everything in between. At the same time, she harnessed her natural ability to put things in order and started organizing her friends' houses on weekends for fun. When word got out in her circle of friends, Jen quickly amassed a six-month waitlist. She realized she might be onto something. When her boss announced his retirement after five years of working together, she took it as a sign and seized the opportunity to launch a full-service professional-organizing business.

While she had no formal business training or experience, Jen credits her entrepreneurial father with instilling in her an incredible work ethic and the capacity to take risks and problem-solve with confidence. Her company motto, "Tell us what you need, and we will find a solution for it," exemplifies Jen's core value of service and her desire to come up with creative answers for common problems. From the get-go, her vision was to serve her home-organizing clients by providing solutions for literally any problem they needed solved. Jen grew her team, recruiting exclusively from within her local community, hiring skilled workers and contractors, as well as new moms and creatives who were thrilled to take on some flexible work. Her small company scaled rapidly, transitioning from a home-organizing

business into a one-stop shop for all things home improvement, with services including hauling, donations and consignment, design, and even custom cabinetry.

Jen eventually divided the business into three separate companies—all thriving and headquartered in Los Angeles, California: Life in Jeneral, her home-organizing business, which includes an impressive roster of high-profile celebrity clients; LIJ Spaces, which offers custom cabinetry design and construction for every room in the home; and LIJ Academy, where she trains and mentors other organizing professionals. In addition to all of that (wait for it!), Jen just published an organizing book, and she has a showroom and full product line in the works. When I ask how on *earth* she is able to manage all of this and stay sane, she credits her Christian faith and the support and influence of her parents, who always encouraged her to help others, live a purposeful life, and strive for greatness. Jen's life and career are a living expression of these values. Everything she's built has been anchored firmly in her faith and her deep desire to act in alignment with her highest purpose and potential. With every step forward she's guided by the question: "How can I help more people?"

JEN'S HOME

Jen shares her spacious and sunny beachfront home with her fiancé and his two children. They've recently merged households (including each of their dogs—both named Charlie!), and for a busy family, the home is surprisingly airy and minimal. I even spot some (gasp!) empty shelves and drawers. Not surprisingly, Jen has employed her signature organizing systems throughout the home to help streamline the space. She takes pride in being a "bonus mom," setting up file bins for each kid to store mementos and using the Artkive app to digitize their art. They converted the garage into a home gym, complete with a custom slat wall (from LIJ Spaces), which perfectly stores their extensive collection of sports gear, helmets, and accessories.

The home didn't come with a walk-in pantry, so Jen created her own stylish and functional pantry zone by adding roll-out shelves to her kitchen cabinets and decanting baking staples and snacks into labeled bins. The two Charlies are a big part of their family life, and Jen has centralized all the dog toys, treats, food, and accessories into a clearly organized zone in her lower kitchen cabinets for easy access. She also loves hosting and entertaining and keeps a fully stocked bar cart in her dining room, so friends can help themselves.

Her walk-in closet in her bedroom is organized by category and color and is spacious enough to display hats and handbags on open shelves. She uses drawer organizers and bins for her daily-use products, which keeps her bathroom tidy and in good shape.

Jen is queen of the problem-solving gadget. During my visit, she introduced me to an expandable cup holder she uses that enables oversize travel mugs and cups to fit securely in her car cup holder (I bought this immediately after I left), a cord concealer for kitchen gadgets, and a rolling tray to make it easy to move her coffee maker and other countertop kitchen appliances. I ask her how she manages loose cords, and she runs to grab a hanging toiletry organizer that she hacked into a cord organizer, where she wraps and secures each cord with a cord tie and stores them in labeled pockets for easy access.

When I ask Jen what her favorite thing is about her home, she smiles and replies, "Can I say the people in it?" The home has a great flow between the kitchen, dining room, and living room with the large front and back windows flung open, making it easy to relax, host, and entertain. Jen loves taking strolls on the beach, using their pizza oven for pizza and movie night with the kids, watching sports while the dogs play in the yard, and having friends over for barbecues and get-togethers. When we talk about her life, she tells me that everything she does, from how she runs her business to how she sets up her home, is rooted in her faith and her desire to cultivate love, community, and connection. "It's not about the house," she explains. "It's about how you make people feel when they're there."

TIPS + TAKEAWAYS

- Create a grab-and-go pet station by corralling pet food, treats, medications, toys, leashes, and bags into one zone. Ditch the packaging and use matching, labeled bins to create a cohesive look.

- Organize your phone-screen apps into groups by color instead of category for an aesthetic that will earn the respect of even your sassiest teenager.

- Repurpose a hanging toiletry bag to create your own organized cord management system. Use cord clips to keep cords tidy and a label maker so you can keep track of what's what.

- To organize tiny toys or accessories, use small bins or pouches to contain items within a bigger container or vessel. Jen calls this micro-organizing!

- There is always a solution if you just take the time to look for one. Do your research and look for creative solutions to common problems.

Q/A WITH JEN ROBIN

WHAT DO YOU LOVE MOST ABOUT YOUR HOME?
I love that it has lots of open space. In the summer we open all the doors in the front and the back of the house, and it's such a wonderful place to hang out as a family. In the winter, we cozy up by the fire and have dance parties at night with the kiddos.

BIGGEST HOME-ORGANIZING CHALLENGE?
We rent, so there are things I wouldn't have done (drawers versus cabinets in the kitchen, for example). There's too little storage in the garage to store the gear for all the activities we do!

WHAT ARE YOU THE PROUDEST OF?
The systems I have created are so easy to maintain for everyone!

DIRTY LITTLE CLUTTER SECRET?
To be honest, I am pretty crazy when it comes to clutter. I maintain the house with my weekly resets and the systems I have created. I can't sleep or do things if the house has stuff all over. However, there's a closet in the garage that has some of the owners' items in it, and that's where we put stuff that didn't work in this space but that we want to keep for a future house.

WHAT IS YOUR MOST TREASURED POSSESSION?
A sprinkle of my dad's ashes that are in an angel necklace I have.

WHAT IS YOUR GREATEST EXTRAVAGANCE?
I love a great-quality handbag that will last forever!

FAVORITE ORGANIZING HACK?
Turning my hanging jewelry travel bag into my tech and cord organizer.

BIGGEST TAKEAWAY OR LESSON LEARNED FROM ORGANIZING OTHER PEOPLE'S HOMES?
Every single client has a unique story and specific needs, so it is important to make sure we are creating a space that is for *them*, so they will want to maintain what we have done. Also, we consume too much as a culture. I always work with clients to break their established consumption and shopping patterns, and I help them identify what's truly important so they won't get into the same trouble again.

WHAT MIGHT PEOPLE BE SURPRISED TO LEARN ABOUT YOU?
That I don't love being on camera and would much rather be behind the scenes than the "face" of LIJ.

WHAT DOES SELF-CARE LOOK LIKE FOR YOU?
Sundays are my favorite days. My version of self-care is cleaning and organizing. I have learned to accept my craziness and lean into it. I love getting massages, facials, and having a date night with Dan.

FAVORITE GIFT TO GIVE?
The 5 Minute Gratitude Journal

GO-TO DAILY UNIFORM?
I'm a jeans-and-tee kind of gal—and a good sneaker.

THE MOST VALUABLE CAREER ADVICE YOU'VE EVER BEEN GIVEN?
FOCUS.

FENG SHUI-INSPIRED IN QUÉBEC

SACHIKO'S STORY

Born in a small town in Alberta and raised in the shadow of the Rocky Mountains, Sachiko was always sensitive to her physical surroundings and drawn to art, architecture, organizing, and design. The oldest of four, she would spend hours making houses and detailed landscapes in the back-yard sandbox her father built. Her parents never had to ask her to tidy her room, and she jokes that she was the geeky kid in class with a perfectly organized desk.

The daughter of a Japanese Canadian father and a Scottish mother, Sachiko credits her practical organizing brain to her mother's side (her grandfather was an engineer) and her attraction to pared-down spaces and minimalist aesthetics to her Japanese heritage. Both parents were very artis-tic (her father studied ceramics and made pottery, and her mother was gifted in painting and flower arranging), so she learned to see the world through an aesthetic lens. Her parents did not have a particular agenda or prescribed path for their children and encouraged them to explore freely. As a result, Sachiko felt the liberty to follow her own interests and passions: She completed a degree in English literature with French language. And she lived and worked throughout France, including a teaching job at a school run by Catholic nuns, where she lived in an old stone house and ate lunch at a long table with the nuns on weekends à la *Madeline*.

Sachiko's career was always varied and interesting: she has worked as a student advisor, a teacher, a self-taught graphic designer, a coach, and an EFT (emotional freedom technique) practitioner. Her coaching work inspired her to further her training with certifications in both feng shui and Marie Kondo's KonMari home-organizing method. Her intuition led her to merge her aesthetic eye and natural organizing abilities with her passion for personal growth and spirituality. The natural next step was to launch a business that married all her passions: a home-organizing and feng shui consultancy designed to help her clients create balanced, intentional, per-sonal, and deeply nourishing spaces.

Her website and stylish marketing cards (initially tacked up on bulletin boards!) attracted clients who were interested in the more soulful and spiri-tual aspects of home organizing. She began working with a wide range of mindful clients seeking harmonious and orderly environments. Her process

evolved into an organic blend of thoughtful decluttering, organizing, spatial planning, layout, and design.

Sachiko also integrates principles of minimalism into her home, life, and work. Her personal definition of minimalism is about choosing to "live lightly on the planet" by being intentional about what we truly need to live a happy life. She tells me, "It's about having a life where we have room to breathe, to truly be present, to see the beauty in simple things, to have freedom to be flexible and spontaneous because we aren't weighed down by taking care of so many material things."

Sachiko is also the proud mom of two creative and inspiring daughters who enjoy setting up their spaces with intention, too! Future projects and dreams include creating online feng shui resources for highly sensitive people (HSP), learning more about bau-biologie (healthy, green, and sustainable living), and finding a piece of beautiful land to build a simple minimal dwelling where family and friends can gather for quietude in nature, community, and slow living.

Sachiko means "happy child" and "good fortune" in Japanese, a name that seems fitting since her business is anchored in the desire to help her clients feel happier and more peaceful in their homes and lives.

LIFE IS SOOO GOOD!

live in the
sunshine,

swim in the sea,
drink the wild air.

EMERSON

SLOW + INTENTIONAL LIVING
= TIME FOR WHO + WHAT I LOVE ♡

F R
WE
A RE
YOUN
& RE E.

SACHIKO'S HOME

Sachiko resides in a sunny two-bedroom apartment in a 1910 historical building on a peaceful and picturesque street in Montreal. Though the apartment needed some love when she moved in, she was won over by the fluid layout, the high ceilings, tall windows, and pretty views. She had a clear vision of what she wanted to create: a simple, bright, Zen-like space filled with plants, simple furnishings, and artwork. She pulled off the transformation on a modest budget, painting the walls and moldings bright white ("Chantilly Lace" by Benjamin Moore), sanding the yellowed floors down to a more neutral tone, swapping out light fixtures and hardware, and adding personal touches, wall hangings, framed textiles, and even a large-scale canvas she painted herself.

She confesses to having high-end tastes with a low-end budget, but she's skilled at sourcing beautiful things in surprising places. She scored a wooden bench and woven rug from her local hardware store and bought her solid wood dining table from Craigslist. IKEA is a favorite source for modern chairs, light fixtures, and bedding. Sachiko has created a beautiful, inviting space without great expense using a harmonious balance of natural, soulful materials (she favors wood, metal, and bamboo).

When I visit her home, I am struck not just by the lovely aesthetics, but how I *feel* in her space. There is a beauty, simplicity, energy, and intention in each room, a feeling of balance and harmony that she's worked hard to create using the five feng shui elements of wood, water, metal, fire, and earth. I am also drawn in by the photos pinned up with washi tape, the collected feathers and small stones perched on a ledge in her entry, and the collection of handmade pottery from her father, who studied in Kyoto, Japan, and made ceramics for much of his life. Her daughter's art is also proudly displayed throughout the home, and even her monthly calendar pinned up in her cheerful office is lovely to look at, with color-coded sticky notes for each activity.

With a nine-hundred-square-foot home, Sachiko also has lots of small-space tricks up her sleeve. Since she doesn't have any storage in her dining room, she uses a rolling bar cart in the kitchen for placemats, napkins, liquor, and tea towels. Instead of large serving platters, she repurposes everyday ceramic dinner plates and bowls for hosting, so she has less to store. Multiple floating shelves and art ledges store objects while taking up less visual real estate. Lots of hooks in her tiny entry closet provide easy homes for keys, umbrellas, tote bags, and purses, and the majority of her wardrobe is neatly file-folded in drawers so she can see her options at a glance. Since she doesn't wear makeup or have a lot of products, bathroom storage is not a big challenge, and her peaceful and minimalist bedroom is furnished simply with an IKEA bed and a set of matching stools that serve as nightstands. The black-and-white prints on her walls were made by her daughter, and I am especially charmed by a black-and-white *OUI, OUI, OUI* graphic she tacked up as decor, found on the internet and printed out for free!

Sachiko describes feng shui as the art of creating nourishing environments where positive energy can flow freely to empower and help us to live our best lives. She says, "I am not a hardcore minimalist, but I tend toward minimalism and intentional living. I find that having less to take care of in my home means having more freedom and time—which for me are the true luxuries."

TIPS + TAKEAWAYS

- Use ledges for displaying found objects such as rocks, feathers, art, plants, and even utilitarian objects, like salt and pepper and oil in the kitchen.

- Repurpose everyday ceramic plates and bowls to use as serving platters so you have less to store.

- Try these easy art hacks: frame fabric swatches or textiles; drape fabric over a wooden dowel; pin up favorite photos, postcards, or printables with washi tape; buy an oversize canvas and paint it yourself to create large scale art on a budget.

- Swap out all the mismatched hangers in your closets—an easy win that instantly creates more visual unity and "feels" both Zen and high-end.

- Place a basket by the front door to drop transitional items into.

- Sachiko recommends placing furniture on a fleecy blanket or towel and sliding it to rearrange furniture without straining your back or scratching your floors.

- See the potential: sometimes a rundown rental just needs to be harmonized and simplified. A fresh coat of paint, some plants, and personal touches can go a long way.

Q/A WITH SACHIKO KIYOOKA

WHAT DO YOU LOVE MOST ABOUT YOUR HOME?
The light, the layout, the high ceilings!

BIGGEST PERSONAL HOME-ORGANIZING CHALLENGE?
Very little closed storage—three very small closets. But I embrace it as a positive constraint that helps me live mindfully with less.

WHAT ARE YOU MOST PROUD OF?
My two beautiful, smart, creative, funny, and generous-hearted daughters.

FAVORITE SPACE TO ORGANIZE?
I especially love when clients move to a new home, and we get to set it up beautifully for them from day one.

DIRTY LITTLE CLUTTER SECRET?
Depends month to month! Life happens, things build up. My main clutter magnet is my phone, where I currently have eleven thousand photos that need to be purged and organized.

CAN'T-LIVE-WITHOUT ORGANIZING PRODUCT?
Sharpie and sticky notes (because I am super visual and have to write everything out), IKEA RISATORP wire-and-wood baskets (because they are cute and versatile with no plastic), and new or repurposed boxes or bins (because they help divide up storage spaces into manageable zones).

GREATEST SPLURGE OR EXTRAVAGANCE?
Sometimes it's a delicious meal out, sometimes it's giving myself work-free days to reset and just "be." More and more, I value having experiences and acquiring fewer, better things.

MOST COMMON MISCONCEPTION ABOUT PRO ORGANIZERS?
That they're always organized—just ask my friends and family how often I have misplaced my keys or my phone or how disorganized I can be with digital things.

ACTUAL MORNING ROUTINE?
I look at the weather forecast, do a mini workout, blend my smoothie, get dressed, and get ready for work. Then I read something inspiring or do gratitudes, pull up Google maps for my client's home address, and head out for some fun!

ACTUAL EVENING ROUTINE?
When I'm ready to wind down, I like to connect by having a little chat with my partner or friends, followed by a hot bath with Epsom salts, then I like to read, listen to music or a podcast, and head off to bed. I love my bed, and I usually fall asleep very fast!

ONE SELF-CARE TIP YOU FOLLOW?
Honoring my body's needs. Taking entire days, as needed, for slowing down when I need to be quiet and recharge. I treat it as an essential reset for body-mind-spirit.

GO-TO DAILY UNIFORM?
Jeans, plain top, Blundstones, little hoop earrings, lapis lazuli ring.

THE MOST VALUABLE CAREER ADVICE YOU'VE EVER BEEN GIVEN?
No one specifically gave me this advice, but I believe in "do what you love." I find this well-expressed by the Japanese word *ikigai*, which is about being connected to our inner passion for life—that thing, whatever it is—that makes us want to jump out of bed in the morning!

WHAT MIGHT PEOPLE BE SURPRISED TO LEARN ABOUT YOU?
Even though my name is very Japanese, my mama was Scottish, and her maiden name was Macmillen. My middle name is Laura, after my maternal grandmother.

A RISK YOU TOOK THAT PAID OFF?
I followed "do what you love" and have been happily self-employed for over twenty years.

STREAMLINED AND SPACIOUS IN THE CAPITAL

RACHEL'S STORY

Type A from birth, Rachel always craved order. In kindergarten she even wrote an entire book about how much she loved to clean and organize. Born in Washington, DC, and the daughter of an attorney, Rachel went prelaw at the University of Wisconsin–Madison, and then immediately received her JD in telecommunications law. She loved studying law, learning how to think critically, and deconstructing contracts, but after dipping a toe into life as an attorney, she quickly realized it was not for her. She made the decision to pivot and used her innate organizing skills to give speeches to law firms on time management and organization. While home organizing was not yet a widely known profession, she mapped out her own course, speaking about organization, leading workshops, taking on individual clients, and even launching a monthly newsletter on organization and productivity. Her consulting services took off quickly, but it was the birth of her identical twin daughters that catapulted her home-organizing business into the spotlight.

After the birth of her girls, Rachel started sharing helpful tips in her newsletter about how to stay organized with twins. A reporter from the *Washington Post* came across her work and asked her to consult on an upcoming story about organizing for multiples. Just weeks after the birth of her twins, Rachel landed a front-page feature in the *Post*, which was quickly picked up by the Associated Press and published nationally. The media exposure led to other opportunities, including television appearances for Rachel and her girls (the twins were very extroverted and loved talking about organization as they got older).

When the kids were in kindergarten, Rachel went through a difficult divorce and became a single parent and the sole provider for their family. Grateful to have an established business and her own income, she credits her organizing business with giving her the ability to comfortably provide for her children, even if it meant a grueling schedule, sometimes even working nights and early before school drop-off. As business increased, Rachel took the leap and built a team (fully composed of other working moms) to keep up with the demand. Most of her clients are busy families, many with multiple homes, looking for full-service support and project management. Rachel's company has become known for its luxury concierge services, including full-service moves, closet design and build-outs, and white-glove home organization for every room in the house.

Rachel now spends the bulk of her time running business operations from her home office and continues to provide organizing presentations for corporate clients. In addition, she offers business coaching for new organizers, online courses, and even a curated product line, including meal planning pads, tote bags, and planners.

A pro with communication, Rachel has continued to leverage her excellent relationships with magazine editors and television producers (with more than one hundred features to date) and has landed significant brand partnerships with companies such as West Elm and the Container Store. A leading expert in the field, she plans on furthering her speaking career and launching a course on how to garner press. While Rachel admits that running your own business is not for the faint of heart, she loves the flexibility that entrepreneurship has provided for her family (she is now happily remarried). She has created a thriving and multifaceted career that supports both her life and her passions. As she tells me with a smile, "Hard work pays off."

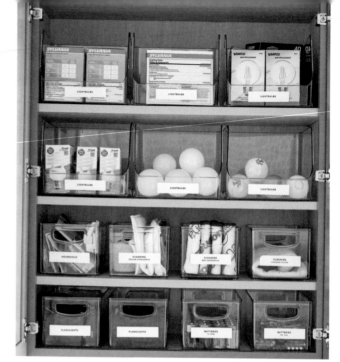

RACHEL'S HOME

The spacious five-thousand-square-foot home that Rachel shares with her husband, Jon, and twin girls is the house that all the kids want to hang out in. Their home is cheerful, bright, and inviting with comfortable family rooms, a homework and art center, the most lovable sheepadoodle puppy, Poppy, and a trampoline in the backyard. The stunning kitchen is well-stocked with cereal, treats, and snacks, complete with a full candy bar at arm's reach in the pantry (I raided it), making the space "teen headquarters" for the twins' many friends. Rachel, who is actually a health nut, jokes that this is by design so that she can keep an eye on them.

RACHEL ROSENTHAL

Rachel's business is known for striking the perfect balance between functional organizing systems and high-end design, and her own home is no exception. In the colorfully wallpapered mudroom, she's centralized the family's high-use items into a sleek labeled system composed of a single cart with drawers and two shelves lined with labeled cloth bins. The drawers and bins create easy-to-use, designated "drop zones" for shop returns, donations, seasonal accessories, sun and bug spray, reusable bags, scarves, hats and visors, swimming and ski gear, and even picnic supplies. On the opposite wall, Rachel has installed hooks for coats and umbrellas above a cubby system, including a row of white, waterproof bins beneath a bench for tucking wet winter boots. The system is designed to ensure success: there are intuitive places to stow all the items that her busy family uses most, which helps keep the rest of the home clutter-free.

Upstairs in the laundry room, a grab-and-go utility station is stocked with lightbulbs, batteries, cleaning supplies, and other household essentials in clear, labeled bins. Rachel personally designed and styled the luxury walk-in closets that are accented with chandeliers, patterned rugs, and other personal touches, including framed childhood photos, books, plants, and art. The lower floor has been converted into a teen-friendly art and homework center, which doubles as a gift-wrapping station. Rachel stores colored pencils, paints, paper, and other arts and crafts in white, labeled bins. Even the home gym is flawlessly organized, with a tall basket for yoga mats, a stand for weights, and a small shelving unit for spin shoes and other workout accessories.

Rachel is queen of the system—she groups similar items together, and each thing has a clearly designated home so that everyone can maintain everything. The entire home is impeccably organized while still feeling warm, welcoming, and comfortable. It's a tough feat to be sure, but Rachel has pulled it off—in style.

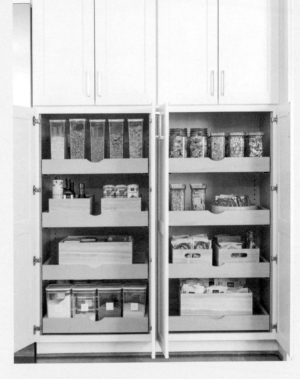

TIPS + TAKEAWAYS

- Use a rolling cart with labeled drawers to make an instant, easy entryway drop station for storing returns, donations, reusable bags, sports gear, and seasonal accessories.

- Create a grab-and-go utility station using open, labeled bins to corral batteries, lightbulbs, furniture pads, and other home maintenance supplies.

- Invest in washable Ruggable rugs, which work well under an art table, or in an entry or other high-traffic areas.

- Empower your children to get a snack for themselves (or better yet, pack their own lunches) by organizing kid-friendly items in the pantry at their eye level for easy accessibility.

- Involve kids in the home-organizing process. Even little ones can sort items by color, test out craft supplies to see what still works, and make handwritten or picture labels (masking tape and marker will do!) to stick on bins, boxes, and shelves.

- Style your closet with art, photos, and treasured objects to personalize the space.

Q/A WITH RACHEL ROSENTHAL

WHAT DO YOU LOVE MOST ABOUT YOUR HOME?
My family and the amazing life we have built together. I was a single mom with my twin girls for a number of years, and the joy of having our complete family with Jon (and, of course, Poppy) together in our home is immeasurable. For the physical aspects of my home, I truly love my closet, the table in our kitchen that we gather around, and the art in our family room from Aspen, Colorado—one of our favorite and most memorable destinations.

WHAT ARE YOU MOST PROUD OF?
My amazing twin daughters and the women they are becoming. I am also (with humility) very proud of myself and the business I have built. I have always strived to be a role model for my daughters, and my hope is that by creating and running Rachel and Company from the ground up, as a single mom, I have given them an example and am a mom they can be proud of.

FAVORITE SPACE TO ORGANIZE?
My favorite space to organize in other people's homes is the pantry. The pantry is the hub of the home, and organizing this space makes such an impact on day-to-day life.

DIRTY LITTLE CLUTTER SECRET?
Skincare and makeup. I am admittedly a lipstick addict and have developed quite the collection. I do my best to keep my beauty products organized but will cop to letting them get a little messy at times.

CAN'T-LIVE-WITHOUT ORGANIZING PRODUCT?
In my opinion the greatest impact products are labels. Having elements organized is one thing, but maintaining the system is another, and labels are the key to that maintenance.

MOST TREASURED POSSESSION?
A photograph I took right after we got engaged of me, Jon, and our twins. You can just feel the love and excitement for our future together as a family of four.

MOST COMMON MISCONCEPTION ABOUT PRO ORGANIZERS?
I think that professional organizers can get a bad rap for not focusing on functionality. In the world of Instagram, a lot of spaces are organized only for the look and not for function. Our team focuses on functionality in conjunction with aesthetics— both are equally important!

YOUR DEFINITION OF ORGANIZED?
Having systems in place that support and improve your daily life by removing chaos and supporting order. Sometimes a perfectly organized space will look like a "normal" house, but it will function well for the family using it.

BIGGEST TAKEAWAY OR LESSON LEARNED FROM ORGANIZING OTHER PEOPLE'S HOMES?
Everyone has similar struggles.

WHAT MIGHT PEOPLE BE SURPRISED TO LEARN ABOUT YOU?
I am an introvert. While I speak in front of large groups, am on social media, do a lot of TV work, and run a team, I can also be shy and reserved.

THE MOST VALUABLE CAREER ADVICE YOU'VE EVER BEEN GIVEN?
Don't compare your business to anyone else's. Look to others for inspiration, collaborate, communicate, and stay your course.

THE DIY DWELLING

ORGANIZED LIVING

JEN'S STORY

Sometimes the worst news can lead to incredible and unexpected opportunities. This was the case when Jen's husband lost his fourth job in five years due to company layoffs—this time right before Christmas. Jen decided to step up and launch her own business to help support her family of six.

But let's rewind. While Jen was growing up in Salt Lake City, Jen's mom taught her how to maintain and keep a tidy and organized home, while her grandmother, who was a designer, sparked her interest in interiors and styling. Jen loved curating beautiful and functional spaces—she was the babysitter who would put the kids to bed and then tidy the house, and her college roommates used to poke fun at her many lists and her color-coded closet. While she has a naturally analytical mind that loves to strategize, Jen didn't realize there was a career that perfectly encapsulated her exact skill set.

Instead, Jen obtained a degree in history and a master's degree in communications. She then got married, started a family, and threw her energy into raising her four children. Her passion for organizing only grew as she refined her skills and simplified her systems to ease the flow of daily life. She also embarked on a passion project with her husband: completely gutting and renovating their first house. Jen personally designed every inch of the home, and the couple completed all of the hands-on work while living there with their four children (it is beyond me how this is even possible). They ripped out the green and orange carpets, painted the walls, learned how to lay tile and refinish floors, and completely transformed the space. It took a full year to complete the makeover, and while Jen confesses that some of the details are far from perfect, the home feels incredibly personal and special.

Upon completion of this massive project in December 2019, Jen's husband unexpectedly lost his job. Finances were tight, and the sudden lack of income left Jen feeling especially vulnerable. She felt strongly called to step up and help her family through this difficult time, so she followed her gut and decided to go all-in on starting a home-organizing business. She read every book on organizing she could get her hands on, built a website, launched a social media platform, and reached out to local designers and influencers to see how she could work with them. She landed a handful of small jobs assisting other organizers and helping designers with styling and staging before finding her own clients. The work came so naturally and easily to her that she

describes feeling like "she was born to do it." As larger jobs arose, she started bringing in friends or family members to help, quickly realizing that with a bigger team she could transform a space in a fraction of the time. She had the idea to scale her team so that in a single day they could declutter, organize, style, and label an entire space from bottom to top. Not one to sit on a big idea, Jen went to work hiring local college students, moms, and empty nesters who loved organizing and turned her garage into a fully stocked warehouse filled with organizing products. Her clients love the quick, transformative results, and Jen's team (she now has more than forty independent contractors!) loves having flexible, satisfying, and creative work.

In addition to the rapid-fire, high-impact makeovers, Jen and her team also offer moving and staging services, custom labels, a "Pinterest Perfect Pantry" online course, and quarterly service projects (free services for women and families), where they give back to members of their community who are struggling through difficult life transitions, illness, or other challenges.

Jen's business growth has already surpassed her wildest dreams, but she now feels like the sky is the limit. Her plan is to create a successful organizing franchise, and she also dreams of writing a book, creating additional online courses, and launching her own product line. "I want to do it all," she laughs. With her husband once again happily employed, it can be challenging to keep up with the demands of a growing business and a busy family, but the

juggle is worth it. Jen has created a thriving, meaningful, and purpose-driven business that has positively impacted her clients, her team, her online community, and loyal fanbase. Among her proudest accomplishments is being able to support, empower, and bring joy to other women. While Jen's business is only a few years old, her growth has been exponential and shows no sign of slowing down. "I just want to serve and give back as much as I can."

JEN'S HOME

Walking into Jen's warm, welcoming home, you'd never guess that she has four kids. Her living room is comfortable and stylish, with throw pillows, plants, art, and even a piano, but no clutter in sight. The secret to keeping her living spaces looking sharp is setting up a drop zone in the garage, with storage lockers for each child, similar to those in a school classroom where everyone unloads their backpacks, jackets, and shoes before they enter the house. She also installed a slat wall system that stores the family's extensive collection of sports gear. Jen claimed the small entry closet for herself, accenting it with cheerful green-patterned wallpaper and oversize baskets for her shoes and seasonal accessories. The open floorplan leads into a dining room with a long table for family meals and a bright, modern kitchen with an island and stools for chatting and snacking. The kitchen is organized to a tee, using the systems, containers, and labels Jen and her company are known for. Each category is carefully zoned, including a baking cabinet; a beverage station fully stocked with coffee, tea, smoothie mixes, and supplements; and her Pinterest-perfect spice drawer.

The small-but-mighty pantry is one of the hardest working spaces in the home. Jen maximized every square inch of vertical space by adding shelving and storing snacks, baking staples, and cooking supplies in airtight jars and uniform bins and baskets. She's also included clever accents such as peel-and-stick wallpaper and a dry-erase board for jotting down grocery lists. She keeps small baskets at arm's reach, stocked with the kids' favorite grab-and-go snacks (I discovered the joy of popcorn chips while visiting).

Jen and her husband share the primary bedroom upstairs, while their kids have their own rooms downstairs. A basket at the top of the stairs collects items that need to be brought downstairs, so they don't clutter the main floor. Jen personalized each of her kids' rooms based on their style and interests, from a swing and floral wallpaper to wall ledges for displaying favorite books and her oldest son's many medals and awards (he's been the top swimmer in Utah for the past five years!). Jen makes it easy to manage daily bed-making (and has eliminated the need to store linens) by investing in Beddy's—an all-in-one washable bedding set that kids can zip up for a neatly made bed each morning. I had to watch a video to fully comprehend it, but it's a gamechanger for her busy family.

The finished basement was converted into a spacious playroom for toys, games, and instruments. Jen added shelves to organize each category in labeled bins that the kids can access on their own. The playroom is complete with a comfy couch and an old-fashioned popcorn machine (!) for movie nights.

With a large family, there is a lot to keep track of. Jen installed a sleek built-in desk across from the kitchen that serves as the family command station. This action-packed workstation has been styled with plants and flowers to make for an inviting place to pay bills, review homework, and file paperwork. Jen has an action basket for items that require attention (no more floating around the house) and easy-access files for taxes, important documents, report cards, and school forms. Designing, renovating, and organizing her home has been a true labor of love. With simple, practical systems and a little daily maintenance, Jen has ensured that her home is always ready for family dinners, cozy movie nights, and quality time with friends and family.

TIPS + TAKEAWAYS

- Add a dry-erase board to your pantry wall or door to jot down grocery lists and meal-planning notes.

- Storage hack: Use a pot rack with S hooks to hang awards, dress-up clothes, and toys.

- Try stick-and-peel wallpaper to spruce up any space on a dime.

- Create a centralized place to store library books by the front door so they never get misplaced.

- Store childhood photos and mementos in binders with clear sleeves (one for each kid), and keep them accessible so they can be enjoyed.

- Create a family command station with folders for each family member and an action-item basket, which can be reviewed each week (Jen has family meetings each Sunday).

- Meal plan on Sundays and place a grocery delivery order for each Monday so each week starts well-stocked with groceries and household supplies.

Q/A WITH JEN MARTIN

WHAT DO YOU LOVE MOST ABOUT YOUR HOME?
It's ours. We have remodeled every corner to be exactly what we want for our family.

FAVORITE SPACE TO ORGANIZE?
Pantries!

DIRTY LITTLE CLUTTER SECRET?
Teenage boys' bathroom.

WHAT'S IN YOUR ORGANIZING TOOLKIT?
Everything an organizer's heart could want! Velcro strips, scissors, label removers, measuring tapes, sticky notes, Sharpies, shelf pegs, cleaning supplies, trash bags, and so much more.

FAVORITE ORGANIZING HACK?
Get rid of bulky packaging and replace with beautiful containers.

WHAT DO YOU DO WHEN YOU FEEL OVERWHELMED IN A HOME OR SPACE?
Just start! I start with the easiest task first and take the project one step at a time. It always ends up working out!

MOST COMMON MISCONCEPTION ABOUT PRO ORGANIZERS?
Our homes are perfectly organized and clean at all times. With four kids and a business I am running, that is not always the case!

YOUR DEFINITION OF ORGANIZED?
A space where everything in it has a purpose and a home.

BIGGEST TAKEAWAY OR LESSON LEARNED FROM ORGANIZING OTHER PEOPLE'S HOMES?
Less is more! Living with less frees up so much mental and physical clutter and creates happier homes and individuals.

WHEN YOU'RE NOT ORGANIZING, YOU'RE PROBABLY . . .
Snow skiing or adventuring with my family.

ACTUAL MORNING ROUTINE?
Exercise, drink my favorite drink, and help my kids get off to school.

ACTUAL EVENING ROUTINE?
Read to and snuggle with my kids, then watch *Friends* with my husband.

ONE SELF-CARE TIP YOU FOLLOW?
Getting outside, eating delicious food, and unplugging.

WHAT KIND OF PLANNER DO YOU USE? HOW DO YOU ORGANIZE YOUR DAY?
Ha! It changes monthly. Still working on finding or creating the perfect planner so I am always trying out any planner I can get my hands on.

WHAT MIGHT PEOPLE BE SURPRISED TO LEARN ABOUT YOU?
I had never shopped at the Container Store until I started Reset Your Nest.

BIGGEST PERSONAL HOME-ORGANIZING CHALLENGE IN YOUR OWN HOME?
Kids. Creating systems that can be maintained for different personalities and different ages has definitely stretched my creativity.

THE MOST VALUABLE CAREER ADVICE YOU'VE EVER BEEN GIVEN?
Write everything down. It took me a long time to take the advice, but writing down every idea, every lesson learned, and everything that works creates a wealth of knowledge that can help with decisions about growth and focus.

A RISK YOU TOOK THAT PAID OFF?
When I decided to bring on other organizers to Reset Your Nest instead of being a one-woman show.

The struggle is real to balance work and home life while maintaining healthy boundaries, especially if you're juggling kids or working from your dining room table or kitchen counter (my hand is raised!). The key is to try to be more intentional about how you set up and maintain your space so you can feel more productive, creative, and in control, both at home and at work. My WFH tips are straight ahead.

STORE IT AT THE STORE

There is no need to overload your space with a massive collection of office supplies, like scissors, Sharpies, paperclips, binder clips, sticky notes, dozens of pens shoved in mugs—or gag gifts from college. Consider what you use and need to work effectively and efficiently, and buy only what you need when you need it.

ELEVATE YOUR ESSENTIALS

An easy and affordable way to elevate your home office is to update the office supplies you use the most. Poppin, Wisdom Supply Co. (totally plastic free), Schoolhouse, and Appointed all carry high-quality essentials designed to help spruce up your space.

PACK IT UP

For those who don't have the luxury of a dedicated home office, I suggest creating a "work-from-home bin," which can serve as a place to corral and contain laptop computers, reference materials, and projects when the workday is done. The key is to stow your work bin in a concealed area (think cabinet, credenza, or storage closet), so your work is out of sight and mind when you're ready to "clock out."

A WORKSTATION ON WHEELS

If your career requires more gear than can be contained in a compact bin, consider turning a rolling cart into your own portable office. You can store everything from cords, AV equipment, books, reference materials, and office supplies neatly on the shelves, and it's a breeze to pack it up and wheel it out of sight when the workday is done.

STOW THE SUPERSIZE SUPPLIES

Consolidate unsightly or oversize electronics into a large credenza, built-in storage cabinet, or utility closet to prevent an eyesore in your home. You might also consider investing in a compact wireless printer that can be easily tucked away (the sleek and tiny HP Tango has my heart).

SAY GOODBYE TO THE PILES

There are few people on this Earth who actually enjoy paper filing, and I do not happen to be among them. Make your life easier by digitizing as much as possible so you can reduce the paper piles and the filing. You may also want to consider a binder system instead of a traditional filing system. Simply group documents in broad categories, and store each category in a labeled binder for easy reference.

THINK OUTSIDE THE PLASTIC SWIVEL CHAIR

When it comes to sourcing furniture and decor for your home office, there's no need to limit yourself to the traditional options, which can feel sterile or generic. Consider sitting in your favorite upholstered comfy chair instead of a plastic swivel chair. Repurpose a regular table as your desk so you can spread out. Add textures and layers like a cozy rug, throw pillows, and art. Make your home office feel like a space you'd actually like to hang out in.

GET CREATIVE WITH STORAGE

There are plenty of household supplies that can be repurposed to create clever organizing solutions for your workspace. A pot lid or letter organizer can be used to dock iPads and laptops. A toolkit or tackle box can serve double-duty as a storage solution for cords, batteries, earbuds, paperclips, or other work-related essentials if you are short on drawer space. You can use a flatware organizer as a drawer insert to keep pens, scissors, and smaller desk accessories tidy.

CONSIDER YOUR SIGHTLINE

If you're sharing your WFH space with others, make sure to position yourself in a way that minimizes distractions from your sightline. If you're working from your dining room table, you probably don't want to be staring at your partner doing the dishes or your toddler playing in the living room. Set up your workspace so that your gaze is as clear of visual distractions as possible.

CURATE YOUR BACKGROUND

Make sure to set up a background you can feel proud of (or at least not embarrassed by) on video calls. A bookshelf or even just a few wall-mounted shelves with brackets can be easily styled using books, plants, art, and pretty objects to create a stylish and professional look.

PLEASE GET DRESSED

As someone who has spent a good deal of time curled up at home writing in pajamas, I've learned that actually getting dressed makes a huge difference in how I feel, act, and show up. A little effort goes a long way here. Take a shower. Brush your hair. Put on clothes that promote how you want to present yourself to the world (they can still be comfortable!). Bonus: You won't have to duck and hide every time UPS shows up with a delivery.

CREATE A CLOSING RITUAL

If you're working from the dining room or kitchen table all day, you may want to try creating a closing ritual that helps you transition out of work mode and into personal mode. Activate your senses in whatever way will help you transition out of the daily grind—clear your work surface, dim the lights or light a candle, spritz yourself with essential oil, or put on your favorite playlist.

CHECK YOUR TECH

Decide what time each day you want to unplug, and make sure you have a designated spot in your home to "check your tech" so you won't be tempted to check one more email or respond to a colleague's texts.

CREATE A DESIGNATED NO-WORK ZONE

Make sure you have at least one area in your home that is not used for work. For example, you may opt to rotate between working from your kitchen island, dining room, and living room, but designate your bedroom for reading, relaxing, and sleeping only. Having a space that is free from devices, cords, and papers can help serve as an oasis—a designated space designed to help you shift gears and get out of work mode.

MINIMALISM GOES MOBILE

XIOMARA'S STORY

How does a maximalist with three hundred pairs of high heels (actual figure, not hyperbole) turn into a minimalist who lives in an Airstream trailer? Xiomara's path to a life with less was far from predictable. Born and raised in San Juan, Puerto Rico, Xiomara describes her childhood as very unstable. She split her time between the houses of her mother, who was very tidy, and her grandmother, whose house was sparkling clean but very disorganized. In addition to relying on outlets such as cooking, singing, and going to church during those difficult years, Xiomara embraced what she'd learned at each home and became a whizz at both cleaning and organizing. Other kids made fun of her fastidiousness, saying she had OCD, but Xiomara associated mess and clutter with instability, so she continued to curate an environment that brought her a sense of stability and peace.

Xiomara's life took an abrupt turn when she became pregnant and had her first child at sixteen. She asked for, and was granted, emancipation from her mother and left Puerto Rico with her baby for the United States. Welfare was never enough to pay for her monthly expenses, so she cobbled together a series of odd jobs to pay for diapers and wipes, even selling the shirt off her back when necessary. Xiomara and her baby lived for short stints with different family members in Orlando, Florida; York, Pennsylvania; Boston, Massachusetts; and Fort Meyers, Florida. She struggled to learn English but was tenaciously determined to finish high school—even with limited resources and a young baby to care for. Shortly after successfully graduating from high school, she gave birth to her second child.

Now a single mother of two, Xiomara moved to Jacksonville, Florida, intent on finding a good job and showing her kids a better life than the one she had known. In Jacksonville, she met and fell in love with Frank, who was eighteen at the time and joined the US Navy shortly after. Frank proposed and legally adopted her two children once they were married. Xiomara trained to become a certified nursing assistant, but once she and Frank had a third child, their combined salaries weren't sufficient to make ends meet. Xiomara was wildly resourceful and found creative ways to supplement her income—for years she resold clothes, tidied homes, and even offered home-made foods, like chocolate-covered strawberries, to bring in some extra money for their family of five. The entrepreneurial spirit was always in her!

Frank continued to rise in rank, and right after their oldest son graduated from high school and joined the military, the rest of the family relocated to Guam for Frank's new post. Xiomara took great pride in setting up their new home, decorating with fresh fruit from the island, neatly folding towels and linens, and storing her growing shoe collection in clear boxes with handmade labels. She loved shopping, and as the couple earned more money and her collection grew, Xiomara meticulously organized and displayed each new item with care. Neighbors would come over to tour every corner of the home like a museum, marveling at how stylish, clean, and organized it was. Family and friends asked why she wasn't a professional organizer or interior designer. Xiomara filed that advice away as something she might consider someday when they moved back home to the continental US, but a chance encounter with a Guamanian woman, who had learned of Xiomara's talent and insisted on hiring her, inspired her to expedite her plans.

Xiomara's youngest son designed her logo, and she figured out the local business laws. She named her new business in honor of her mother, Lilly, whom Xiomara credits for her organizing process. Through her signature grit and determination, the home-organizing business was launched within twenty-four hours, and before long she was booked solid just through word of mouth and referrals.

One day something abrupt and strange happened to Xiomara that changed her life. All her stuff, including the clothing and shoes that she'd amassed and that had always been a source of joy for her, started to give her a headache and make her feel physically ill. In that moment she made the decision to start dramatically downsizing. She started by paring down her jewelry collection. Next, she tackled her three hundred pairs of shoes. Then came clothing. She sold some but it was taking too long, so she ended up giving most of it away—she needed it out of her life as quickly as possible. After a few months of sorting, selling, donating, and giving away most of the things she owned, Xiomara looked in the mirror and wept tears of joy. She felt like she was seeing her authentic self again, the little girl from Puerto Rico who loved singing and cooking and simple pleasures.

The new happiness and freedom she felt was not instantly contagious. Her husband and sons felt connected to their stuff and considered their belongings part of their personal history and memories, so they resisted joining her decluttering effort. When her middle child graduated from high school and moved out to join the service, the family downsized to a smaller home, transitioning from a 3,500-square-foot penthouse to a 1,200-square-foot condo. Xiomara continued selling and donating, intent on further simplifying her life and paying off years of accumulated consumer debt. Once her youngest son graduated from high school and went off to join the service (two of her sons now serve in the air force and one on border patrol), Xiomara urged Frank to make a dramatic lifestyle shift and pare down even further. The empty nesters seized the opportunity to start a new chapter in their lives. They sold most of their possessions, paid off all their consumer debt, and invested in a two-hundred-square-foot Airstream based in San Diego, California, which they now happily call home.

When Xiomara reflects on how minimalism changed her life, her face lights up: "Minimalism has helped me discover my authentic self and better connect to my family. I feel so free now—free from clutter, free from the pressure to buy things to impress other people, free from judgment." Paring down to the essentials and simplifying their lives has afforded the couple more time to enjoy each other and a greater quality of life. They now have a deeper and more intentional appreciation for their surroundings and the present moment.

Living in a home that is mobile means that Xiomara is able to bring her services to literally anyone in the country and provide support to people who may not have access to professional organizers or organizing products otherwise. She is passionate about her work and its impact.

XIOMARA'S HOME

When I meet Xiomara and Frank for the first time, their Airstream is parked in a beautiful and lush mobile community in Chula Vista, California. A sign secured to the front door of the Airstream reads "small house, big welcome," and the couple does not disappoint. While Xiomara shows me around their home (affectionately referred to as Noa, the Puerto Rican Airstream), Frank works on hand-chopping wood and building a fire, so he can help prep the lunch they have planned for our visit. Their dog, Scooter, curls up in the custom sleeping nook Frank created in the Airstream under their bed. The tiny home has been thoughtfully organized and customized, enabling the couple to store everything they need at arm's reach. Their entire wardrobes occupy only two narrow rows of cabinets. Xiomara, the same woman who once owned more than three hundred pairs of shoes, now has a total of eight pairs stored in cloth bags and tucked neatly into two small bins above her bed, alongside a few sets of pj's. There is a hanging closet rod in the shower, but it's seldom used—the couple doesn't own any formal or fussy attire, opting to rent, buy secondhand, or borrow as needed instead of storing things they will seldom wear.

The interior space is so tiny and minimal that I find myself spontaneously peppering Xiomara with a hundred questions about where things are stowed. Toiletries and makeup? Everything from Q-tips to nail polish to first-aid supplies have been neatly gathered into clear, labeled bins and stored on the two narrow shelves above the bathroom counter. Office and organizing supplies? They're above the dining table in built-in cubbies zoned into neat vertical bins. Suitcases? They opt instead for compact backpacks for travel and tuck them under the bed next to their extra blankets. Sentimental items? Xiomara has a single teddy bear from her son tucked away in her nightstand, but she's digitized their lifetime of photos, videos, and letters and given the originals to her three children. Jewelry? She only owns a few items inherited from her mother, which she wears and cherishes. This includes one set of daily earrings, one for special events, and two heart charms (one in red, her favorite color, and one in gold). And three watches—one a gift from her mom when she turned eighteen, one given to her the last Christmas her mother was alive when she was thirty, and one she bought for herself.

Xiomara and Frank affectionately refer to the back of their truck that pulls their Airstream as "the garage." The small storage space houses their two bikes, two small generators, a grill, a toolbox, folding tables for organizing projects, paddleboards, and solar panels. To stay fit, they take long walks and do jumping jacks outside (my kind of exercise—no gear required!), and when I look around in search of winter coats or rain boots, Xiomara laughs and tells me they've managed to be just fine without the bulky seasonal items that most people own. "If we need something, we can always get it," she assures me.

Despite the minimal lifestyle, their tiny home is not short on personal touches. The bedroom is adorned with an entire wall of framed photos from the couple's twenty-year wedding anniversary. Xiomara loves to celebrate holidays by decorating the home inside and out and has managed to fit all of

her decor into a single bin the size of a shoe box. She also loves styling with greenery, investing in plants that are easy to care for (air plants, succulents, snake plants) but also splurging on fresh flowers weekly.

The compact kitchen is outfitted with all the cooking essentials they need for daily meal prep, including a small but well-stocked pantry (complete with a full set of spices, fresh produce, and Frank's favorite breakfast bars), a wall-mounted knife set, a few pots and pans, and just two sets of dishes, glasses, and mugs (they use compostable versions for guests). Xiomara shows me the tiny hand-crank coffee grinder she uses for their daily cup and pulls out the felt dividers she uses to carefully wrap plates and glassware when they hit the road to prevent breakage. The Airstream community is known for sharing small-space hacks and resources, and the couple loves swapping their tips with other Airstream dwellers.

Owning a tiny home doesn't hinder their ability to cook, host, and entertain. Their dining area comfortably seats four and can convert into a cozy sleeping area for two guests. When extended family is visiting, they can set up folding chairs and socialize around the fire or relax at picnic tables. They take great pride in their Puerto Rican culture and cook together daily, rarely opting to eat at restaurants. During our visit, Frank grills perfectly seasoned steak, while Xiomara whips up a full feast of beans, rice, salad, and sliced avocados. It's cold and windy so they crank the heat, and we enjoy a relaxed meal together inside the cozy home. Immediately following, Frank takes out the trash and recycling, and Xiomara tidies up and resets the space.

Sharing a tiny home with a partner is not for the faint of heart, but these two seem to genuinely love being together—cooking, watching movies, taking long walks, connecting with the tiny-home community, and maintaining their beloved home, fully embodying the "less house, more home" ethos. Xiomara's career is in full bloom, and Frank, who recently retired after twenty-two years of service in the US Navy, is happy to assist his wife when she needs an extra set of hands. The morning after our visit, they hit the road to drive east, living out Xiomara's dream of organizing homes across the country. It strikes me that they seem remarkably relaxed with such a huge trip on the horizon, but then I realize they have no real prep to take care of. There's no mail to pause, no pet sitters to line up, no suitcases to pack up. Just the open road, adventures ahead, and everything they need and love at arm's reach.

TIPS + TAKEAWAYS

· Want your family to get on board with a minimalist lifestyle? Start with your own stuff. Xiomara thoroughly edited her own wardrobe and personal items before her family was inspired to join the decluttering effort.

· Invest in products that have dual functions. In the Airstream, a macrame hanging fruit basket doubles as paper-towel holder, a charming, space-saving solution.

· Customizing countertops with laminate is not just inexpensive and easy to remove—it's a great way to try out a new look without committing to something permanently. Frank and Xiomara covered their dark countertops with a light laminate to test a new look without breaking the bank.

· Digitize memorabilia and important documents. Xiomara stores all of the family memorabilia digitally on a website (with backup on a hard drive).

· Rent or borrow special occasion clothing that you will only wear once so you have less to store and maintain.

Q/A WITH XIOMARA ROMERO

WHAT DO YOU LOVE MOST ABOUT YOUR HOME?
It's tiny and shiny.

BIGGEST HOME-ORGANIZING CHALLENGE?
Downsizing from 3,500 square feet to 200 square feet.

WHAT ARE YOU THE PROUDEST OF?
My minimalist journey.

WHAT IS YOUR MOST TREASURED POSSESSION?
My mom's jewelry.

YOUR DEFINITION OF ORGANIZED?
Everything in its place, and a place for everything.

MOST COMMON MISCONCEPTION ABOUT PRO ORGANIZERS?
That we are a cleaning service.

WHAT DO YOU DO WHEN YOU FEEL OVERWHELMED IN A HOME OR SPACE?
Thankfully I have never felt overwhelmed in any home or space.

WHAT IS YOUR GREATEST EXTRAVAGANCE?
Maintenance of my nails.

WHAT'S IN YOUR ORGANIZING TOOLKIT?
Label maker, masking tape, markers, basic tool kit, wipes, trash bags, miniature dustpan with brush, and snacks.

WHEN YOU'RE NOT ORGANIZING, YOU'RE PROBABLY . . .
Spending time with family, cooking, or enjoying the outdoors.

BIGGEST TAKEAWAY OR LESSON LEARNED FROM ORGANIZING OTHER PEOPLE'S HOMES?
To always make time for your own self-care.

BEST ADVICE FOR ASPIRING ENTREPRENEURS?
Be yourself no matter what.

WHAT MIGHT PEOPLE BE SURPRISED TO LEARN ABOUT YOU?
That I'm more of an introvert than an extrovert.

HOW DO YOU ORGANIZE YOUR DAY?
I use a small calendar on the fridge for basic scheduling, and I use a pen and notebook for more in-depth scheduling.

WHAT DOES SELF-CARE LOOK LIKE FOR YOU?
Quiet, alone time to meditate and reflect on myself.

ACTUAL MORNING ROUTINE?
Coffee and meditation walk.

ACTUAL EVENING ROUTINE?
Watching a show or movie with my husband.

THE MOST VALUABLE CAREER ADVICE YOU'VE EVER BEEN GIVEN?
Do it while you're scared; don't wait till things are perfect because they may never be.

A RISK YOU TOOK THAT PAID OFF?
Starting my business while I was still living overseas in Guam. No one knew what a professional organizer was, and there weren't any on the island.

HOW DO YOU RECHARGE WHEN IT'S ALL TOO MUCH?
Unplug and reset with some quality family time. They are always there to help.

FAVORITE GIFT TO GIVE?
My time and a home-cooked meal.

GO-TO DAILY UNIFORM?
T-shirt with my logo, a pair of jeans, and my only pair of sneakers.

TÂNIA LOURENÇO

AN URBAN RETREAT
IN HISTORIC LISBON

TÂNIA'S STORY

The circumstances of Tânia's life have led her to several different countries, and while her identity is firmly rooted in her African heritage, she feels she "belongs to the world." Tânia was born in Luanda, Angola, during a civil war. Her father believed she would have a better life under the care of her aunts and uncles in Lisbon, Portugal, so she was sent to live with them when she was four years old. She lived in Portugal for five years before returning to Angola to reunite with her parents.

Aside from keeping her personal things tidy, there were few early signs pointing to a future career as a home organizer. In high school, Tânia dreamed of going to law school so she could represent underprivileged individuals and communities, but she ended up following a different path. After receiving a full scholarship to study biochemistry in the United States at Indiana University, she fell in love, graduated with a degree in microbiology, and returned home, where she got married and had her first daughter (she now has two daughters).

Eager to continue her education, Tânia was accepted into the MBA program at the University of Oklahoma, where she focused her studies on marketing and healthcare management. Her husband had to remain in Africa for work, so Tânia completed her master's degree with her baby in her arms (and in the classroom). After years of study and multiple degrees, Tânia returned to Angola, where she landed a position as a microbiologist in a subsidiary clinic. She was quickly promoted and eventually was made the head of the department of occupational health and safety. After two successful years in the position, she asked to be transferred to a different subsidiary, where she became the head of the department of quality and environment in an industrial economic zone. Soon after, Tânia's youngest daughter was diagnosed with an immune disorder, so the family relocated to South Africa, where the air and the healthcare system were much improved. South Africa proved to be politically turbulent and often violent (Tânia personally witnessed many episodes of great violence), so the family decided to move once again. This time they chose Ottawa, Canada, where her in-laws were living and where her daughter could receive excellent care at a reputable children's hospital. Only three months later, Tânia's husband was transferred to Belgium for a work assignment, so once again they uprooted to start over in Europe.

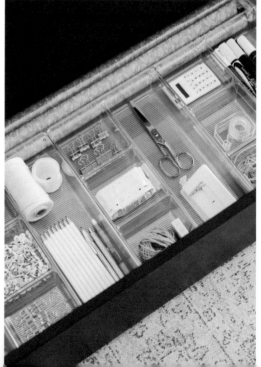

The following years proved challenging. With her husband working all the time, Tânia found herself alone in a new country, mostly spending time at home caring for her daughters, one of whom was still quite ill. She had always been an inherently organized person, and during a particularly difficult period, she instinctually started creating order and systems within her home to help her feel more in control of her life. During this time, she was inspired by looking at the Neat Method website (see pages 49–51). Eager to connect with a community of professional organizers, Tânia joined the Professional Organizers in Canada (POC) and began taking classes over the telephone. The professional-organizing skills she learned felt intuitive to her, but despite her many professional accomplishments in other fields, Tânia felt insecure and nervous about becoming a traditional home organizer. Instead she focused on meticulously transforming her own home and documenting her progress on Instagram. While she never cared for social media, Tânia was motivated to share her experiences with the hope to inspire other women who might also be struggling in their own lives. She started by organizing her refrigerator, accenting it with fresh, cheerful flowers. Then she moved on and tackled other common clutter culprits, like her laundry room, pantry, and closets. Unlike traditional home organizers who spend their days in other peoples' homes, Tânia focused her energy on using her own home as a laboratory and sharing her successes and tips online. Her strategy proved successful, and her work caught the attention of brands across the globe who reached out to partner with her.

She has quickly amassed a huge global audience who love her warm, empathetic approach and stylish, colorful aesthetic. Today she lives in Lisbon and consults with both individuals and global brands who love her signature style and aesthetic. She is still pursuing the same singular goal that she had when she started—inspiring and helping other women to manage challenging life transitions. With another possible move on the horizon, you can be sure to expect plenty of real-life tips, content, and more inspiration from Tânia's home and life ahead.

TÂNIA'S HOME

Tânia doesn't consider herself a minimalist but rather someone who really doesn't like shopping. Since she's used to moving frequently, it's tremendously liberating to live with fewer belongings. Less stuff is easier to manage on a daily basis and a cinch to pack up and transport. I visit her in Lisbon, where she's recently created a new home in a beautiful old neighborhood called Aloma. It's a walkable neighborhood surrounded by local pastry shops (she treated us to pastel de nata fresh out of the oven!), markets, cafés, and parks. Her daughters, Nuria and Anya, (now a tween and a teen) attend the local French school nearby and are fluent in French, Portuguese, and English.

Unlike most family entryways, Tânia's is nearly empty. A slim IKEA shoe storage unit (popular with other organizers) stows shoes by the front door, and a handful of hooks provide storage for bags. Tânia explains that the girls know to take their backpacks to their room, so there's not much to store.

Beyond the entry, the two bedrooms are so sparse I wonder if everyone has fully unpacked yet. They have. It turns out the entire family is super minimal, especially with their clothing, a by-product of moving so often. Tânia's slim wardrobe holds fewer than a dozen items (she does laundry daily), and her daughters' shared closet unit has (gasp) empty drawers. In the drawers, they use bookends to secure file-folded items, which prevent them from falling over. The sisters store games and books in the "library" in the hallway and keep games in pouches to avoid wrestling with broken cardboard boxes. They've converted a spare room into a cheerful workspace for art, homework, and projects. Nuria is a talented artist and musician, and Anya loves to follow her mother's lead, meticulously organizing her drawers and shelves (can we all have an Anya in our homes, please?).

Tânia doesn't have a dedicated home office, preferring to work on the sunny patio, so she's created an "office-in-a-drawer" in the living room. Clear drawer dividers separate supplies, chargers, and cords in a display that would make Martha Stewart proud. Other household supplies are stored neatly in the laundry room, which Tânia wallpapered herself to make it more cheerful and inviting. Matching white bins contain detergent, spare vacuum parts, and cleaning supplies, while mini Command hooks are used for hanging the beautiful wood-and-leather fly swatter she brought from Belgium and her favorite broom from France.

Tânia spends most of her time in the kitchen, and it shows. She loves to cook and has mastered the art of the beautifully organized food pantry. Nonperishable items, like pasta and grains, are decanted into clear glass jars and labeled with a chalk pen, cereal and kid snacks are stored at arm's reach in clear canisters, and her favorite beverages brought over from Belgium are organized by flavor in stylish white-and-wood baskets. Tânia is well-known for her cheerful food styling, and she does not disappoint. Her narrow refrigerator opens to display an array of rainbow-colored fruit, which she preps weekly for her kids to snack on. Beverages are decanted into glass bottles, meats and cheeses in stackable clear containers, and eggs are lined up in a ceramic crate. The pièce de résistance is a small bouquet of fresh flowers, which lasts longer in the fridge and is also lovely to look at. She keeps her proteins and vegetables in the freezer in individual reusable silicone bags, and food storage containers are accessible right above the fridge, so it's easy to pack up leftovers. Her cabinets display her collection of beautiful Portuguese ceramics and glassware, which the family eats off daily instead of saving them for a special holiday or event.

At the end of our visit, we celebrate with an ice cream–bar toast (I'm thrilled to see her collection of Magnum bars organized in a bin in the freezer—a woman after my own heart), and I get to meet her bunnies, Oreo and Pancakes. It's love at first sight for me, but the bunnies are more interested in hopping around. Tânia explains with a laugh, "Bunnies really like their routines. They're worse than organizers."

TIPS + TAKEAWAYS

· Keep food storage containers close to the refrigerator for easy grab-and-go access. Tânia likes to separate storage containers used for hot food and leftovers from containers for fruit and dry goods so they don't leave smells or flavor behind.

· Use a pot lid organizer to separate and organize reusable food storage bags.

· Stackable drawers are a functional under-the-kitchen-sink solution for storing dishwasher soap and cleaning supplies and can also help hide unsightly pipes.

· Hot tip: Storing fresh flowers in the fridge at night will help them last longer. Bonus? They're lovely to look at, even stored in the fridge!

· Pick designated days to shop and meal prep. Tânia shops on Friday and does all of her meal prep on Sunday so she's ready for the week ahead.

· Drawer divider alternative: Repurpose bookends to keep file-folded clothes in place in your dresser.

· Try a nonstick drawer liner in the kitchen to arrange utensils instead of trying to puzzle-piece together drawer dividers that will magically accommodate that pesky potato masher.

Q/A WITH TÂNIA LOURENÇO

WHAT ARE YOU MOST PROUD OF?
My first under-the-sink cupboard project. I was able to bring my vision to life.

FAVORITE SPACE TO ORGANIZE?
Hands down everything in the kitchen, especially small pantry cupboards.

CAN'T-LIVE-WITHOUT ORGANIZING PRODUCT?
Glass jars, bins, and baskets.

MOST TREASURED POSSESSION?
Memories I've been creating with my daughters.

FAVORITE ORGANIZING TIP OR IDEA?
Be selective when organizing a small space (let's say a pantry). Instead of six types of pasta, you may only be able to keep two, and it's okay. You should adapt to the space you have, not the other way around.

WHAT DO YOU DO WHEN YOU FEEL OVERWHELMED IN A HOME OR SPACE?
I declutter first. Most times an overwhelmed reaction to a space has to do with the number of things that are in that space, not necessarily with how clean the place is.

MOST COMMON MISCONCEPTION ABOUT PRO ORGANIZERS?
That pro-organizers' homes are never untidy.

YOUR DEFINITION OF ORGANIZED?
To have systems compatible to the house and to the family that lives in it, where objects in the house have homes and can easily be stored after each use.

BEST ADVICE FOR ASPIRING ENTREPRENEURS?
Walk the journey of entrepreneurship with a partner; it's a lot easier as long as you choose the partner wisely.

ONE SELF-CARE TIP YOU FOLLOW?
Drink warm lemon water first thing in the morning and sleep at least seven hours per night.

THE MOST VALUABLE CAREER ADVICE YOU'VE EVER BEEN GIVEN?
If you need to take a chance in life (business- or career-wise), take it now; it gets harder with age. The older you get, the less courage you'll have to start something new.

BIGGEST TAKEAWAY OR LESSON LEARNED FROM ORGANIZING OTHER PEOPLE'S HOMES?
If your energy is not good at a certain point in time, avoid organizing other people's homes.

WHEN YOU'RE NOT ORGANIZING, YOU'RE PROBABLY . . .
I love to have a great chat with my daughters over an afternoon snack at our kitchen table, and I also enjoy walks in the park and cooking.

ACTUAL MORNING ROUTINE?
Wake up, pray, wash, drink warm lemon water, unload the dishwasher, prep young child breakfast and school snack, feed pets, do a load of laundry, wake up kids, get dressed, drop kids at school, have breakfast, work.

ACTUAL EVENING ROUTINE?
Exercise while supervising pets, help kids with homework, remove clothes from line, prep young daughter's next day's outfit, cook dinner, have dinner with family, load dishwasher, watch TV with kids, water balcony plants, lay down with youngest daughter, work in bed, review next day's to-do list, kiss my daughters good night, sleep.

WHAT MIGHT PEOPLE BE SURPRISED TO LEARN ABOUT YOU?
I've lived in six countries, on three continents, and speak four languages.

WARM MINIMALISM IN PORTLAND

DEVIN'S STORY

Devin's story is one of rebirth and renewal. Raised by progressive parents in a small town in Kentucky, the Southern values of basketball, God, and horses were as ingrained in her as the rolling bluegrass fields. She never felt like she belonged there, but she learned to be strong in her convictions and values, even when they were different.

Devin found independence in the nearest "big city" of Cincinnati, where she studied psychology and went on to pursue a master's degree in clinical mental health counseling, but ended up leaving before completing her last semester. She and her then fiancé, Jess, had decided to move west after visiting Portland once. They fell in love with the weather, food, landscape, and progressive values and decided it was everything they wanted.

They could take only what fit in a U-Haul, so they sold all their possessions except for their beloved Tempur-Pedic mattress. This dramatic downsizing effort became a catalyst to reevaluate everything. Devin started questioning the brands she invested in, the products she consumed, and even the people she allowed into her life. Intentionality, sustainability, and authenticity became the new guideposts for all decision-making, and Devin became passionate about supporting brands that had a proven commitment to sustainability, ethical practices, and a reduction in plastic and packaging waste.

In addition to feeling more joyful, calm, and empowered, the lifestyle shift enabled her to release her attachments to emotional shopping and ultimately become debt free. Her personal transformation sparked a new entrepreneurial vision. A single post on Facebook asking if anyone was looking for home-organizing support led to her very first clients. She quickly developed her own style and methodology, which integrates not just decluttering, organizing, and styling but also intuitive coaching, visualization, intention setting, and energy healing. Sage clearings, crystals, and reiki (she's certified in Holy Fire reiki) are frequently incorporated into her process to help her clients fully reset and transform their spaces. She admits she initially felt the need to conceal her passion for energy healing and alternative modalities, but now these skills are what set her business apart from traditional professional organizers.

Her holistic approach has attracted a wide range of clients, including artists, creatives, and entrepreneurs. Devin's background in psychology and mental health infuses and informs every aspect of her work, from clarifying goals to navigating long-held attachments. A personal journey toward a more authentic and intentional life has given her the tools to inspire, support, and encourage others to do the same. She has been able to merge her passions for energy healing, sustainable design, and mental health into a fulfilling and meaningful career, using her personal brand of coaching and organization to create calm in her clients' homes and lives.

DEVIN'S HOME

Though Devin's home with Jess and their two dogs, Piglet and Sampson, is a rental, nothing has deterred her from carefully customizing every square inch. Highly sensitive to her environment, Devin has always had a clear vision for how she wants her space to look, feel, and function. Instead of living with generic details found in many rental properties, she's added her personal touch and style simply and cost-effectively. This includes refreshing dull walls with a new coat of paint, removing doors to make the small home feel airier and more spacious, and swapping out each light fixture, as well as the hardware and door pulls throughout the house. To conceal the dark teal vinyl on the entry floor, she laid down patterned contact paper and placed a rug over it. She also used this clever trick with contact paper to transform the unsightly backsplash, counters, shelves, and drawers throughout the kitchen. To create a calm and neutral environment, Devin sourced textiles and art with rounded, soft edges and added throw rugs in warm desert neutrals to draw attention away from the rental's drab carpet.

In addition to updating the bones of the house, Devin has carefully sourced and curated every item in the home (even utilitarian items, like her cooking utensils and salt and pepper shakers, are in her signature warm neutrals color palette). She loves supporting local Portland-based brands (Cedar & Moss, Sandbox Ceramics, and Abby Williams Studio are among her favorites), and she also discovers small and emerging artists through the Etsy marketplace—her one-stop shop for everything from art to hardware.

The couple originally moved into a seven-hundred-square-foot home in Portland, so they've acquired loads of small-space hacks along the way. In the kitchen, spices are stored in magnetic containers and mounted on the side of the fridge, freeing up valuable cabinet space, and even the tiniest drawer is fully optimized by ditching all packaging and installing drawer dividers. Investing in multipurpose products is always a space-saving win, and Devin has even discovered a single appliance that serves as an air fryer, toaster, and mini-oven in one. Mind blown! In the bathroom, she's customized every detail, installing a stylish towel holder and modular drawer organizers that contain her curated selection of daily-use products. In the linen closet, additional wall-mounted shelves maximize the vertical space and make it possible to store backup products, linens, and other household essentials grouped by type in stylish baskets. The couple's bedroom contains only a bed and the single dresser they share (file-folding all garments helps maximize space). When I ask how they get by without a single nightstand, Devin points me to a small basket tucked discreetly under the bed that stows nightly essentials and reading. Her minimalist tendencies serve her well in a small home with less stuff to store and manage. She invests in a single set of jersey sheets for the winter and swaps out with linen for summer, and she and Jess own just two towels each. Fun fact: In signature Portland style, despite the frequent rain, you won't find umbrellas or rain boots in this home, although Devin does employ a SAD light for natural light during the long, overcast winters.

Jess is neurodivergent and doesn't crave the same sense of order and tidiness that Devin relies on to feel good, but they've arrived at a brilliant solution for successfully sharing a small home and have thoughtfully divided up the space to account for each person's needs. Devin has designed and maintains the shared living spaces and bedroom to her taste and specifications, while Jess has full rein over the garage and small bonus room. Jess's room is painted bright yellow and packed full of clothes, shoes, and personal objects. The garage houses a gym, DJ gear, bikes, and two shelves containing pet and camping gear, house paint, tools, and gardening supplies. Jess has plenty of designated personal space for unwinding, hobbies, and projects, while Devin can enjoy the calm, minimalist aesthetic she's become known for both personally and professionally.

TIPS + TAKEAWAYS

- Refresh your rental: Customize and personalize your home by laying contact paper over ugly vinyl; swapping out light fixtures, towel hooks, and hardware; and giving dull or dingy walls a fresh coat of paint. A fun DIY lighting trick? Spray paint an IKEA light fixture or picture frames for a custom look on a budget.

- Budget-friendly art doesn't have to be bland. Source unique, printable digital art from Etsy, and use IKEA frames for an affordable, polished look.

- Dual-purpose products for the win! Opt for multipurpose beauty products (such as a lip-and-cheek tint or an SPF-foundation combo), as well as appliances that perform multiple functions.

- Make it magnetic: Spice jars, small storage canisters, and even a paper-towel holder can all be mounted onto your fridge to help maximize space in a tiny kitchen.

- Up-level the utility items: Source kitchen utensils and salt and pepper shakers in your preferred color palette to feel cohesive with the rest of your home's aesthetic.

- No nightstand? No problem. Use your window ledge to prop up reading glasses and lotion, and tuck a small basket under the bed for stowing other nighttime essentials.

Q/A WITH DEVIN VONDERHAAR

BIGGEST PERSONAL HOME-ORGANIZING CHALLENGE?
Lack of storage in the kitchen.

WHAT ARE YOU MOST PROUD OF?
Doing what I love for a living and truly helping people live more authentically.

FAVORITE SPACE TO ORGANIZE?
Pantry.

DIRTY LITTLE CLUTTER SECRET?
Every space goes through waves but tends to be fairly organized by the next day. As organized as I am, I do hate cleaning!

CAN'T-LIVE-WITHOUT ORGANIZING PRODUCT?
Woven baskets!

WHAT IS YOUR MOST TREASURED POSSESSION?
I'm definitely not a sentimental person, so this is a tough one! A few childhood photos and a shirt that once belonged to my closest relative are very special to me.

WHAT IS YOUR GREATEST EXTRAVAGANCE?
Food and home decor, and a lot of self-care too. I'm a Taurus through and through!

WHAT DO YOU DO WHEN YOU FEEL OVERWHELMED IN A HOME OR SPACE?
Remove visual clutter first.

BIGGEST TAKEAWAY OR LESSON LEARNED FROM ORGANIZING OTHER PEOPLE'S HOMES?
People are fascinating, incredibly creative, and make meaning in their lives through deep connection with others. Everyone has a story. I learn just as much (if not more) from every client I work with as they do from me.

WHEN YOU'RE NOT ORGANIZING, YOU'RE PROBABLY . . .
Hiking—nature is my church.

MOST VALUABLE CAREER ADVICE?
Start before you're ready. To me, entrepreneurship is like that scene in *Indiana Jones* where you have to trust and let yourself fall, and then a step appears to catch you on the way down. Everything works out, even if it's not the way it was originally envisioned. And sometimes it's even better.

FAVORITE GIFT TO GIVE?
I like to give my time and share experiences with people, but I rarely give physical gifts. Lately I've been gifting all my clients a subscription to Ridwell (a local recycling subscription service).

WHAT KIND OF PLANNER DO YOU USE? HOW DO YOU ORGANIZE YOUR DAY?
Ink+Volt has been my favorite for three or four years now. I live by my physical and digital calendars. I schedule anything that requires my best brain power (sessions and meetings) in the morning between 7 to 11 a.m. Afternoons are more relaxed, and I end the workday by 3 to 4 p.m.

A RISK YOU TOOK THAT PAID OFF?
Moving across the country and starting a new life with no safety net was definitely a risk. Starting my business and going all in with no other income sources from the start was a risk, and sticking with it through the pandemic was definitely a risk, but all of those decisions have led me here. Helping people is my soul work; it's what I'm meant to do.

GEORGIA LEWIS

AN ON-THE-ROAD AUSSIE'S PIED-À-TERRE

GEORGIA'S STORY

For her fortieth birthday, Georgia celebrated by spending six months in India. By this time, she had already found a way to see much of the world on her own, traveling to countries including Russia, China, Laos, Thailand, New Zealand, Morocco, Argentina, and Mexico, as well as adventuring across the United States, Canada, and Europe.

Born in Sydney, the daughter of an English father and Australian mother, she spent her childhood enjoying time in London, England, for holidays with family and taking frequent ski trips to Aspen, Colorado, with her mother. After graduating from university in Sydney, Georgia moved to London for a postgraduate degree in marketing, while simultaneously working in sports marketing. She spent her days managing sports celebrities and athletes, organizing everything from their hectic calendars, travel, and logistics to brand partnerships. Her work was stimulating and very detail-oriented, making use of her inherent ability to organize anything. As a child she had fought a constant losing battle trying to organize her room-mate sister, who was far less interested in order.

Georgia next moved on to work in Hong Kong for an ATP (Association of Tennis Professionals—don't worry, I didn't know either) tournament, and after winning the green card lottery, she realized another childhood ambition and moved to Manhattan to work in advertising. After three years working in New York, she landed a dream job with the Aspen Film Festival, and she made Colorado her home base for the next full decade.

Despite having a stable career and home in Aspen, Georgia continued to prioritize travel as a foundational part of her life. She took on a public relations gig for New York–based author and designer Carolyne Roehm, which enabled frequent trips back to New York and regular visits with friends and family in both Sydney and London. On these trips she always found herself home organizing for friends and family. It was only after Marie Kondo's global success that Georgia realized a career could be born of her favorite pastime. As her passion for transforming spaces surpassed her desire to stay in public relations, she decided to make an official career pivot and launch her business: Happy Life Styling, a boutique home-organizing consultancy.

Business took off quicky and grew via word of mouth. It was an easy and natural fit for Georgia, who loved the work and especially the tight

bonds she formed with her clients. "It sounds corny, but I really like making a difference. My most rewarding moments are when I know I've changed someone's life, home, or routine for the better, and my work will impact so many other areas of their life."

Georgia's marketing background came in handy with creating her website, which shares dramatic before-and-after photos from her work. She has leveraged her networks in Sydney, London, New York, and Aspen to grow a small but steady roster of clients who wanted Georgia to "happy life" their homes. Georgia's somewhat nomadic lifestyle hasn't been a hindrance to business—in fact it is one of the keys to her success. Currently splitting her time between Sydney, London, New York, and Aspen (as well as frequent jaunts to explore other countries), she has cultivated a loyal client base that is delighted to work with her. Georgia has created a life and career on her own terms, calling the shots and following her passion.

With the unique goal of traveling to three new places a year, the next countries on her bucket list include Uzbekistan, Lebanon, and the Maldives. One thing is certain, Georgia's wanderlust shows no sign of waning, and all roads continue to lead to travel. For this globe-trotting home organizer, every day is an adventure.

GEORGIA'S HOME

In her signature spontaneous style, Georgia has hopped on a plane from the United States to arrive in London just forty-eight hours before our photo shoot. She had been wrapping up a large organizing job in Connecticut but managed to finish the project and secure a lovely furnished rental in London through a family member in time for our arrival. The flat, where she plans to stay for the next season or two, is in a historic regency-style building from the early 1800s in a charming neighborhood called Maida Vale. The area is often referred to as Little Venice because of the nearby canals. The home is surrounded by cafés, restaurants, and lush tree-lined foot paths. Georgia's temporary apartment is only 580 square feet but feels quite airy and spacious due to the soaring high ceilings and tall windows. While some of the very modern furniture, art, and decor isn't her style, she quickly made the space feel like home by immediately "happy life-ing" each room (code for organizing and styling in her signature fashion) only hours after arriving in London. She laments that she couldn't reach a few of the highest bookshelves in the living and dining space but was able to personalize the lower shelves using books and plants and a few of her beloved collected items and treasures like the tiny tiki statue from New Zealand. She also added her unique touch to the kitchen, clearing counters and repurposing jars she found in the cabinets to decant and artfully arrange her pantry staples. She is accustomed to getting scrappy with whatever organizing and styling products she finds when traveling. A mini shoe rack and single stool make up the entirety of the tiny entryway, which poses no real challenge since Georgia travels exceptionally light. A light packer myself, I insisted on deconstructing her tiny carry-on, eager to glean her best packing tips.

Georgia keeps many of her possessions (including her car!) under the watchful eye of close friends and family around the world, collecting them only when she needs them. Since she's typically on the go, all she needs is a single carry-on suitcase stocked with a handful of versatile wardrobe staples to suit the season. When we meet in London in springtime, she's packed an assortment of casual separates and light dresses that are easily paired with her trench coat and simple flats or sneakers. On cold or rainy days, she's ready with a mini travel umbrella and a single warm, cozy scarf (a cashmere version from MUJI for inquiring minds). Among her must-have travel essentials, she includes her compact laptop computer and chargers, a pack of international adapters and cords, her three passports, water bottle, pillbox, and organizers for toiletries and jewelry. Everything is packed into neat little cubes that puzzle piece together perfectly in her compact carry-on. She also swears that her Longchamp travel duffel is ideal for filling with new treasures or souvenirs. Anything she purchases is carefully considered: "Do I want to lug this around with me?" Typically, she opts out and thus has less to tote around.

Although she has just arrived in London, her flat already feels comfortable, and Georgia seems completely at ease. We walk to lunch in the rain to a nearby eatery surrounded by a lush, green plant nursery and return to chat and warm-up with a cup of tea. She tells me that the very first thing she does when she arrives in a new city is unpack her suitcase. Once her toiletries are set up in the bathroom, pj's are laid out on the bed, house shoes are arranged by the door, and the kettle is on for a cup of English tea she feels instantly settled. Her next adventure will take her to Athens and then to Sicily, but she's not worried about making friends or starting from scratch in a new city. After all, she says, smiling, "I can make a home anywhere."

TIPS + TAKEAWAYS

- Pack like a pro: Use compression packing cubes to maximize space in your suitcase, wear your heaviest items on the plane, and follow Georgia's advice—always travel with a mini umbrella.

- Travel tip: Even when packing light for a trip, bring a compact duffel to load up with treasures, souvenirs, or even dirty laundry. Georgia opts for the Longchamp Le Pliage Original Travel bag, which rolls into a compact bundle and doubles as a chic handbag.

- All that glitters: Add a single metallic item, like a gold blouse or a sparkly shoe, to easily elevate even the most basic wardrobe. Georgia dresses quite simply in versatile staples but finds a little sparkle can go a long way in feeling dressed up when necessary.

- Ask yourself before buying something new: "How would I feel lugging this around or having to get rid of it later? Is it worth it?"

- Identify a few habits or personal items that make a new space feel like home. Georgia loves unpacking immediately in a new space and always brings a few treasures from her travels so her new space feels personalized on arrival.

Q/A WITH GEORGIA LEWIS

BIGGEST HOME-ORGANIZING CHALLENGE?
Logistics and where I'll be for summer and winter, which means I don't always know what can stay in one hemisphere and what needs to come with me. I often find myself having to buy the same thing twice, which goes completely against my minimalist principles.

WHAT ARE YOU MOST PROUD OF?
Personally, my lifelong friendships. Professionally, my before-and-after shots and all the stories behind them.

FAVORITE SPACE TO ORGANIZE?
Oh, that's hard. I love doing laundry rooms because they're often overlooked yet used nearly every day, and I try to use plants whenever possible to make the space feel less utilitarian.

DIRTY LITTLE CLUTTER SECRET?
I really can't think of any, but the trunk of my car often resembles a mob scene at a Container Store Thanksgiving sale.

WHAT DO YOU DO WHEN YOU FEEL OVERWHELMED IN A HOME OR SPACE?
Breathe. Then I break the space down into parts. I also remind myself that it's not brain surgery I'm performing!

MOST COMMON MISCONCEPTION ABOUT PRO ORGANIZERS?
That we scan and judge any residence we're in. We don't! I do often start moving furniture in my head, but it's more a challenge for myself than a judgment of the owner.

YOUR DEFINITION OF ORGANIZED?
Being able to locate something on the spot. Therefore, it's not always about throwing things away but about having storage systems that make sense and making the best use of the storage space that you have.

BEST ADVICE FOR ASPIRING ENTREPRENEURS?
Forget about nine to five and view every conversation you have as a potential client pitch, whether it's friends of friends, your bank manager, or a sales assistant.

BIGGEST TAKEAWAY OR LESSON LEARNED FROM ORGANIZING OTHER PEOPLE'S HOMES?
The problem of too much stuff is universal.

WHEN YOU'RE NOT ORGANIZING, YOU'RE PROBABLY . . .
Trying to improve my golf handicap.

ACTUAL MORNING ROUTINE?
Five-minute meditation, English breakfast tea, emails, all with the radio on—I mainly listen to UK radio wherever I am in the world.

ACTUAL EVENING ROUTINE?
No such thing . . . I'm not usually in the same place long enough to get in a set routine.

GO-TO DAILY UNIFORM?
For work, black and/or white . . . something I can climb a ladder in if needed, but never active wear. Slip-on shoes, as I always take them off before entering someone's house.

ONE SELF-CARE TIP YOU FOLLOW?
Nails—a manicure instantly makes me feel like I'm back in control!

WHAT MIGHT PEOPLE BE SURPRISED TO LEARN ABOUT YOU?
That I am the most last-minute, unplanned traveler—my packing is organized and minimalist, but my preparation, research, and hotel bookings are almost nonexistent.

SARIT SELA

SIMPLE AND SCANDI
IN STOCKHOLM

264   ORGANIZED LIVING

SARIT'S STORY

Our homes and environments shape our days, our lives, sometimes even our careers. This was the case for Sarit, who was born and raised in Nahariya, a small town in northern Israel that borders Lebanon. As one of four siblings, she happily assumed the role of mother's little helper. She loved organizing and put herself in charge of doing and folding laundry for the entire family (she's welcome in my home anytime). Even as a child, she embraced all aspects of homemaking, voluntarily deep cleaning the home each week to help her family prepare for Shabbat (again, always welcome in my home).

After finishing her required Israeli military service and getting married, she obtained a law degree at her father's urging but knew within months of law school that life as a lawyer was not a fit for her. Instead, she chose to move with her husband to a suburb of Tel Aviv to work for her father's metal-working business. Sarit loved learning all about business operations and spent the next two years organizing every aspect of the business and workspace. She created systems for the printing heads and mechanical parts that her father manufactured, and she managed all aspects of the company, including overseeing orders, inventory, and operations. It occurred to her that organizing was her greatest strength, but it would take years for her to discover it as an actual viable profession.

When Sarit was pregnant with her second child, her husband, Daniel, asked if she would consider moving to Stockholm for him to pursue an exciting work opportunity. She agreed and the couple found a beautiful apartment in the city center to rent. At first they didn't know anyone in Sweden, but Sarit loved being home with her children and found calm and joy in all aspects of motherhood. She enjoyed comforting rituals, like leaving candles in the windows and cozying up with warm blankets and hot beverages. She also took pleasure in creating a beautiful home for her family and discovered her love of design, influenced by the city itself. Scandinavian style, characterized by clean, minimal lines and a seamless merging of functionality and beauty provided endless inspiration. Sarit used her own home as her laboratory, and as her kids grew and became more independent, she was itchy to reestablish her own career. At this point she had lost her beloved mother to ovarian cancer and then underwent the removal of her own ovaries as a preventative measure, abruptly ending her fertility and the dream of having more children.

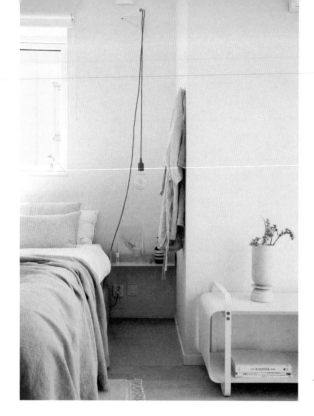

She became seasoned in the art of letting go, grieving personal losses while also discovering the joy of owning less.

She had been aware of Marie Kondo's book *The Life-Changing Magic of Tidying Up*, but when she stumbled upon an opportunity to become an organizing consultant through the KonMari program, she finally found her true calling. Sarit immediately flew to London to train as a consultant, and soon after she launched her business, officially turning her passion for minimalism, design, and organization into a profession.

Sarit learned quickly that the Swedes were not fully on board with the home-organizing craze (she speculates it's related to being an independent, do-it-yourself culture), but her community back in Israel was eager to learn about everything from Marie Kondo's methodology to Scandinavian design. Sarit flew back and forth on low-priced flights to Tel Aviv, taking on clients, leading workshops, and even creating a signature talk: KonMari, Minimalism, and Everything in Between. She also began sharing photos of her home, life, and travels on Instagram and within a year had reached 30k followers. Approached by brands and other consultants who wanted to tap her expertise, Sarit began offering business and brand consulting services, as well as content creation. When the COVID-19 pandemic began, she was fortunately well-poised to run an exclusively online business. She refocused all her energy to content strategy and creation, as well as virtual business mentoring, courses, and seminars on topics including home organization, KonMari, and Instagram strategy for business owners.

SARIT'S HOME

Sarit's airy home is a joyful celebration of Scandinavian design. The space is defined by clean lines, a neutral palette, and smart, stylish storage solutions around every corner. Look closely and you'll find personal treasures sprinkled everywhere: dried and pressed florals, beautiful ceramics, and a few sentimental items, like a pig figurine Sarit jokingly purchased for her husband (it travels with them to every home).

Nearly all the furniture and accessories in the home were sourced locally from Sarit's favorite shops in Stockholm (I was lucky enough to get a design tour!), as well as more affordable options from the Swedish outposts of MUJI, Zara, and H&M Home. Her home is bright, airy, and minimal— a study in muted, neutral tones with a few pink and tan accents, creating a cohesive aesthetic. Sarit jokes that her bright red hair provides more than enough color, so neutrals rule the day both in her home and her wardrobe.

The home opens to a narrow entryway adorned simply with wooden hooks for coats and bags, a tiny two-tier shoe rack, and deep drawers that conceal the rest of the family's shoes (note to self: find a way to add deep drawers in our entryway). The sunny living and dining rooms are clutter-free, proving that when there is less stuff, there is less to organize and everything is easier to maintain, even with a busy family of four.

In the kitchen, Sarit celebrates her favorite artists and designers with beautiful ceramics by Israeli artist Ronit Yam, and bowls, plates, mugs, and glassware from ARKET in Stockholm. The food pantry is composed of a handful of shelves, displaying the family's staples in clear glass jars arranged neatly on wooden trays. A single pull-out drawer beneath the sink holds compost, recycling, trash bins, dishwasher pods, and a beautiful cleaning brush. Household utility at its finest!

The bedroom Sarit shares with her husband is her favorite room, and she's poured her energy into sourcing her favorite lighting, linens, and decor.

She loves to layer soft linen and muslin bedding, which adds texture and warmth to her minimalist style, and she's added sweet details, like postcards propped up on her nightstand, a few favorite books, and ceramic vases with a single dried flower. Just above the staircase, a compact wall-mounted desk unit (a common storage solution in Sweden) has been installed, creating a stylish and functional work-from-home space in the bedroom. On the desk sits nothing more than a laptop, a few decorative objects, and two monogrammed leather storage boxes for supplies (a gift from Danish company August Sandgren). A small closet area is impeccably organized and displays all the clothes, shoes, bags, and accessories with a simple wardrobe rack for current wardrobe staples.

Sarit's kids each have their own simply decorated bedrooms with a few small treasures and keepsakes propped up on their window ledges. I learn that the secret to maintaining tidy teen rooms is to store all books, games, backpacks, clothes, and mementos in their closets with doors that close. Massive floor bins are filled with LEGOs that can easily be tucked back in the closet when the day is done. When it comes to art and schoolwork, the kids pick their own selections to keep each year and store the favorites in a handful of binders in their respective closets. This is a simple solution that empowers them to make their own decisions while minimizing paper clutter.

All the bedrooms in the home have the same white, taupe, and oatmeal layered linens and soft muslin duvet covers, which achieve a wabi-sabi perfectly unperfect look (ideal for kids and teenagers who rarely prioritize a neatly made bed). The guest room is a perfect retreat for family and visitors, with nothing more than a bed, a single nightstand with a reading lamp, and an inviting stack of magazines on the floor.

In the pastel-toned linen closet (one of Sarit's very favorite spaces), she makes household utility aspirational. Sheets, towels, and blankets are file-folded into neat bundles, and linen napkins, face towels, and tablecloths are arranged in wooden storage boxes and stacked neatly on shelves. The raw space only contains white metal shelving, but Sarit's thoughtful styling and calming color palette transform the space and make it pleasing to the eye.

During my visit, I learn so much about the Nordic lifestyle. I'm stunned to learn that the sun goes down in winter as early as 2 p.m. and charmed to hear that the Swedes are known for lighting candles and leaving them to twinkle in the windows to add some much-needed light during the darkest days. As Sarit tours me through Stockholm, I notice how elevated even utilitarian objects are in this city—from brooms to fire extinguishers to scrub brushes. The design details are meticulous and inspiring, marrying form and function without sacrifice. It's easy to understand how the city itself has informed Sarit's home, and her home has become the foundation and inspiration for her work and career.

After ten years in Stockholm, Sarit's husband was offered a new work opportunity, this time in Copenhagen. When we met, she was days away from a large relocation with her family. When I asked if she would be sad to leave Stockholm, the city which informed so much of her creative work and career, she shook her head. Stockholm provided her with years of creative inspiration and the foundation to start her creative business, but she was eager for a new landscape and opportunities. Just as Stockholm informed her style, perspective, and even career, Copenhagen is certain to spark more creativity. "I can't wait," she said. "I'm ready for new inspiration."

TIPS + TAKEAWAYS

· Use dried florals to accent your home—a sweet touch that requires zero upkeep and maintenance.

· Embrace nature in the home. Sarit's son displays a single pinecone he found in Israel on his window ledge and her daughter has a collection of rocks on her desk.

· Want to create a minimalist home that doesn't feel cold or stark? Add warmth and texture by layering in textiles, throws, and pillows. Sarit prefers soft muslin and linen fabrics that look intentionally wrinkled and relaxed and are family- and dog-friendly.

· Install slim, vertical storage solutions to maximize space in a small room. Sarit's workspace consists of a slim desk unit with a few shelves that tuck into the tight space above the staircase.

· Try setting up a "single sock basket" in your laundry room so when you stumble upon a stray sock, you can easily find a match.

· Install deep drawers for shoe storage in the entryway to prevent an eyesore by the front door.

Q/A WITH SARIT SELA

BIGGEST HOME-ORGANIZING CHALLENGE?
My walk-in closet!

WHAT ARE YOU MOST PROUD OF?
That my teenage daughter is organized and a minimalist like her mom!

FAVORITE SPACE TO ORGANIZE?
Wardrobes and kitchens.

DIRTY LITTLE CLUTTER SECRET?
Outdoor storage.

CAN'T-LIVE-WITHOUT ORGANIZING PRODUCT?
No such thing.

MOST TREASURED POSSESSION?
Probably my mother's jewelry (although I never wear it).

GREATEST EXTRAVAGANCE?
My furniture.

WHAT'S IN YOUR ORGANIZING TOOLKIT?
Myself only! I keep it simple and only work with what my client's house has to offer.

FAVORITE ORGANIZING TIP OR IDEA?
The KonMari folding method.

MOST COMMON MISCONCEPTION ABOUT PRO ORGANIZERS?
That we are actually house cleaners.

YOUR DEFINITION OF ORGANIZED?
Living only with the things that spark joy and letting go of all the rest.

BEST ADVICE FOR ASPIRING ENTREPRENEURS?
Always follow your intuition.

BIGGEST TAKEAWAY OR LESSON LEARNED FROM ORGANIZING OTHER PEOPLE'S HOMES?
People always complain that they don't have enough storage space, but the truth is that they simply have too many things.

ACTUAL MORNING ROUTINE?
5k run.

ACTUAL EVENING ROUTINE?
Always a shower before bed.

ONE SELF-CARE TIP YOU FOLLOW?
Since my mom passed away seven years ago, I run.

A RISK YOU TOOK THAT PAID OFF?
Investing a lot of money on my website.

HOW DO YOU RECHARGE WHEN IT'S ALL TOO MUCH?
I organize! It relaxes me.

FAVORITE GIFT TO GIVE?
Always prefer an experience than an actual item.

WHAT KIND OF PLANNER DO YOU USE? HOW DO YOU ORGANIZE YOUR DAY?
Everything is organized in my head and in Google calendar.

WHAT MIGHT PEOPLE BE SURPRISED TO LEARN ABOUT YOU?
I don't drink and never wear jewelry or perfume.

GO-TO DAILY UNIFORM?
Oversize wool coat (because it's always cold in Sweden) and sneakers.

THE MOST VALUABLE CAREER ADVICE YOU'VE EVER BEEN GIVEN?
Always have a clear vision, and don't let people make your journey blurry.

Across the board, there were many overlaps in the habits, practices, and philosophies of the professional organizers I interviewed for this book. Read on for a roundup of easy, actionable tips you can employ to organize your home like a pro.

OWN FEWER LINENS

One of the things that shocked me the most was how minimal most organizers are when it comes to the quantity of linens they own. We're talking one to two sets per bed max. Owning less means less to launder, fold, and store. If you're short on storage space, this is a major victory. Ditto for the towels. Toss 'em. And by "toss," I mean keep your favorites and donate the rest to your local animal shelter or textile recycling center.

DITCH THE PACKAGING

Fast track to making your home look like it was touched by a professional organizer? Ditch the packaging! Get that toilet paper out of its plastic wrap. Remove printer ink from its cardboard packaging. Shop the bulk bins, and pour pantry staples into airtight glass jars. Less is always more when it comes to plastic and cardboard packaging.

MAKE IT A STATION

If there's one thing that is guaranteed to make an organizer giddy, it's centralizing frequently used items into a dedicated zone or "station." Think breakfast station, smoothie station, pet station, homework station, work-from-home station— the possibilities are endless.

MOVE IT, SHAKE IT

Organizers love to get creative when it comes to redesigning spaces: moving furniture around; repurposing bookshelves, dressers, or credenzas; adding, subtracting, or adjusting shelves; installing wall-mounted or over-the-door solutions. Customize your space to fit your needs.

THE DISPLAY AND CONCEAL RULE

Organizers love to *display* items that are lovely to look at, like vases, ceramics, framed photos, plants, and art, on open shelves. We love to *conceal* utilitarian items, like charging cords, tools, house paint, vitamins, and first-aid supplies, in bins, drawers, or deep storage.

STYLISH STORAGE

Whether repurposing or sourcing new products, the pros like to be highly intentional when it comes to storage vessels. Choose bins, baskets, boxes, and organizers that create a cohesive aesthetic throughout your home and reflect your personal taste and style preferences.

SHOP YOUR HOME FIRST

Most pros like to "shop" their client's homes before hitting the stores. Most people have an assortment of bins, baskets, boxes, pouches, and other vessels that can be repurposed for all sorts

of organizing and storage needs. If you do need to fill in some gaps, make sure to shop with a specific list and a plan (note quantities and measurements) before you hit the shops.

ELEVATE THE MOST NEGLECTED SPACES

It's easy to overlook styling in the tucked away areas of your home, like your linen closet or laundry room, but pro organizers take great pride in sprucing up the hidden spaces behind closed doors. Elevate your own utilitarian spaces by adding plants, art, textiles, stick-on patterned wallpaper, or even just a coat of fresh paint. Organizers also love styling closets with design books, candles, and pretty objects found elsewhere in the home. Get creative and give the spaces behind closed doors a little love.

PUT THINGS AWAY, RIGHT AWAY

If there's one habit all organizers can agree on, it's simply to make it a routine to put things back after use to prevent a massive pileup (and headache) later. A five-minute tidy before bed is another common practice of the pros.

RESPECT THE PHYSICAL BOUNDARIES OF YOUR SPACE

As Ryan from Home + Sort says, "Don't shop for a mansion if you live in a cottage." Organizers like to embrace and celebrate the space they have.

CONCLUSION

I've seen firsthand that organization has the power and potential to help people improve their lives on every level. An organized home doesn't just look good, it generally translates directly into less stress, less friction and fighting with the people we live with, less frustration over losing things, and less shame about missing bills and deadlines. An organized home creates a sanctuary in which you can relax, a space in which you're proud to host others, and more efficiency, ease, time, money, and energy for the things you truly care about. Who wouldn't want that?

While the organizers included in this book have diverse stories, backgrounds, and even methodologies, they are united by the desire to help others live more purposeful, intentional, and joyful lives. In sharing their homes and highlighting their tips, tools, and ideas, my intention is both to inspire people to make positive changes in their homes and lives and to show that there are many different paths to get there. Perhaps you want to add some joyful pops of color and personality to your storage spaces like Tinka. You might be motivated to reduce your environmental footprint and set up a sustainable pantry like Wiebke. Maybe you want to start downsizing so you can pay off debt and lighten your load like Xiomara. This book was designed to be a choose-your-own-adventure resource you can return to again and again as your interests, circumstances, and priorities shift. I hope that you'll mix and match the tips and tricks that resonate for you and customize new systems and routines that will work in your home. Start small: Set up a donation bin. Cut the plastic. Clean out a drawer. Solve a problem. Design hacks of your own that will make your life easier.

Most importantly, before you do anything else, take some time to clarify what's important and how you want to live. Organization is simply a tool—a process and practice. It's a means, but it is not the end. My wish for you at the end of your organizing journey is more spaciousness, more breathing room, and more freedom and flexibility to spend time on the important stuff—whatever that may mean for you.

Happy organizing!

ACKNOWLEDGMENTS

Sharing what's under your kitchen sink with a bunch of strangers is kind of like parading down the street naked. This book is in your hands today because of the generosity, candor, and vulnerability of the twenty-five people profiled who trusted me enough to open their homes and tell their stories and let me snoop around their medicine cabinets and peek inside their pantries.

I'm forever indebted to the following people: Vivian Johnson, my long-time collaborator and friend, who trekked around the globe with me and stayed at a few questionable motels during a pandemic to capture the images in this book. My beloved literary team—my agent, Julia Eagleton; editors, Kim Keller, Dervla Kelly, Ashley Pierce, Michelle Hubner, and Rita Madrigal; art director, Betsy Stromberg; production manager, Serena Sigona; marketer, Andrea Portanova; and the entire team at Ten Speed Press. Thank you for your continued cheerleading and guidance, and for believing in and supporting my vision for this book. I'm so grateful.

A huge bucket of gratitude to Tinka Markham Piper, Leila Nichols, and Laura Fenton for their editorial support, candid advice, and friendship. My always-supportive inner circle of friends and family for being the best humans in all the ways. You know who you are.

To Jordan, always, for everything. My daughters, Chloe and Emilie, for making me laugh more than should be allowed and reminding me to put my computer away. I'm free now, let's hang out.

READY TO GET ORGANIZED?

I encourage you to explore the services and programs of the talented experts featured in this book. You can also visit www.shiragill.com for free resources, online courses, and custom consultations.

THE ORGANIZERS' DIRECTORY

BRITTANI ALLEN, PAGE 174
Atlanta, Georgia
www.pinchofhelp.com
@pinchofhelp

HOLLY BLAKEY, PAGE 100
Alamo, California
www.breathingroomhome.com
@breathing.room.home

NIKKI BOYD, PAGE 38
Charleston, South Carolina
www.athomewithnikki.com
@athomewithnikki

LAURA CATTANO, PAGE 58
Brooklyn, New York
www.lauracattano.com
@laura.cattano

JENNIFER DU BOIS, PAGE 134
San Diego, California
www.organizedbyjend.com
@organizedbyjend

JULIEN FEBVRE, PAGE 70
Paris, France
www.julien-home-organizer.com
@julienhomeorganizer

JEAN GORDON, PAGE 80
Wilton, Connecticut
www.jeangordonstyle.com
@jeangordon.style

ASHLEY JONES, PAGE 90
Houston, Texas
www.ashleyjones.co
@ashleyjoneshatcher

SACHIKO KIYOOKA, PAGE 194
Montreal, Québec, Canada
www.soulfulsimplicity.life
@soulful.simplicity

BRANDIE LARSEN AND RYAN EIESLAND, PAGE 162
Sacramento, California
www.homesort.org
@homesort

GEORGIA LEWIS, PAGE 254
London, England
www.happylifestyling.com
@happy.life.styling

WIEBKE LIU, PAGE 144
Oakland, California, and London, England
www.blisshaus.com
@blisshaus

TÂNIA LOURENÇO, PAGE 234
Lisbon, Portugal
www.homganize.com
@homganize

MARGARIDA MADEIRA, PAGE 154
Torres Novas, Portugal
www.homedearhome.pt
@doula_das_casas

TINKA MARKHAM PIPER, PAGE 18
Montreal, Québec, Canada
www.solvemyspace.com
@solvemyspace

JEN MARTIN, PAGE 214
Salt Lake City, Utah
www.resetyournest.com
@reset_your_nest

ASHLEY MURPHY, PAGE 48
Chicago, Illinois
www.neatmethod.com
@neatmethod

FIONA NURSE, PAGE 124
Vancouver, British Columbia, Canada
www.fionanurse.com
@fndinteriors

MARIE QUÉRU, PAGE 28
Paris, France
www.larrangeuse.com
@larrangeuse

JEN ROBIN, PAGE 184
Los Angeles, California
www.lifeinjeneral.com
@lifeinjeneral

XIOMARA ROMERO, PAGE 224
Mobile across the United States
www.lillysorganizing.com
@lillys_organizing

RACHEL ROSENTHAL, PAGE 204
Bethesda, Maryland
www.rachelrosenthal.co
@rachelorganizes

SARIT SELA, PAGE 264
Stockholm, Sweden
www.minimalist-me.com
@minimalistmeblog

CLAUDIA TORRE, PAGE 110
México City, México
www.organizarte.mx
@organizarte

DEVIN VONDERHAAR, PAGE 244
Portland, Oregon
www.themodernminimalist.biz
@the.modern.minimalist

ABOUT THE AUTHOR
AND PHOTOGRAPHER

SHIRA GILL is a globally recognized home-organizing expert, speaker, coach, and lifestyle creator with a less-is-more philosophy. She has helped thousands of people around the world reduce clutter and create more space for what matters. Shira's books center around the intimate relationship between people's homes and lives and how they inform and inspire each other. Her work and home have been featured in *Vogue*, *Dwell*, *Better Homes & Gardens*, *House Beautiful*, *Architectural Digest*, *Domino*, *Forbes*, *Goop*, *Harper's Bazaar*, *HGTV*, *InStyle*, *Parents*, *Real Simple*, and the *New York Times*. Her bestselling book, *Minimalista*, has been translated into multiple languages and implemented by readers around the world.

www.shiragill.com
@shiragill

VIVIAN JOHNSON is a California-based interior lifestyle photographer with an eye for capturing lived-in spaces, architectural details, and interesting personalities. Her years as an award-winning photojournalist taught her how to tell a memorable story that truly captures the soul of the spaces people design and inhabit. Her work has been featured in publications including *Architectural Digest*, *Luxe Interiors + Design*, *California Home+Design*, *Dwell*, *Forbes*, the *Wall Street Journal*, the *New York Times*, and *Real Simple*. Vivian is the photographer behind several books, including Shira's first book, *Minimalista*.

www.vivianjohnson.com
@vivianjohnsonphoto

Minimalista

Your Step-by-Step Guide to a Better Home, Wardrobe, and Life

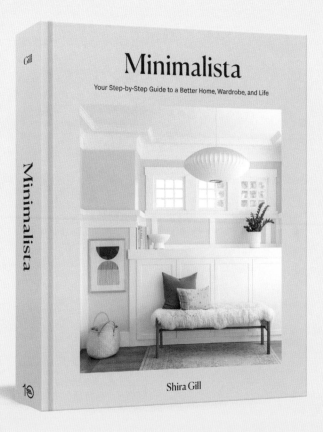

"This book is the resource, encouragement, and inspiration you need to create a home you love today and keep you on track in the future."

—NATALIE WALTON, international bestselling author of *This Is Home*

"*Minimalista* will help you find your dream home beneath the clutter. This book is an indispensable guide for anyone who wants to pare back to what is essential and let go of the rest."

—LAURA FENTON, author of *The Little Book of Living Small*

DESIGN CREDITS

Front Cover Featured Home: Holly Blakey

Back Cover Featured Homes: Laura Cattano, Marie Quéru, Shira Gill

Image opposite page 1: Interior Design by Cindy Ngo for Ink and Porcelain

ART CREDITS

Page 16: Rachel Castle

Page 18: Cath Laporte

Page 20: Rachel Castle, Judit Just (textile), and Nathalie L'été

Page 22: Ara Osterweil, Rachel Castle, Hayley Sheldon, and Lisa Congdon

Page 23: Rachel Castle, Graça Paz, Sam Markham, Ondine Crispin, and Hayley Sheldon

Page 25: Rachel Castle

Pages 60, 62: Ilka Kramer for Tappan Collective

Page 73: Amit Shimoni

Page 80: Lillian August

Pages 83, 84, 85: Michael Gordon

Page 126: David Itulu

Page 144: Gerhart Hermeking

Page 157: Graça Paz and Cinzia Ghigliano

Page 198: Rachel Castle

Page 212: Weaving by Audrey Cowan

Page 244: 252. Real Fun, Wow!, and Abby Williams

Page 247: Real Fun, Wow!, and tumble

Page 258: A. Bilu

Page 259: J.E.L.

Page 262: Roy Conn

Text copyright © 2023 by Shira Gill LLC
Photographs copyright © 2023 by Vivian Johnson

All rights reserved.
Published in the United States by Ten Speed Press, an imprint of Random House, a division of Penguin Random House LLC, New York.
TenSpeed.com
RandomHouseBooks.com

Ten Speed Press and the Ten Speed Press colophon are registered trademarks of Penguin Random House LLC.

Typefaces: Fontfabric's Noah Groteque and Fontsmith's FS Brabo

Library of Congress Cataloging-in-Publication Data

Names: Gill, Shira, 1977- author. | Johnson, Vivian (Photographer), photographer.
Title: Organized living : solutions and inspiration for your home / Shira Gill ; photography by Vivian Johnson.
Description: California : Ten Speed Press, [2023] | Summary: "Get inspired to level up your home organization with tips, worksheets, Q&As, and photos of the living spaces of twenty-five international home organizers, from the author of Minimalista"— Provided by publisher.
Identifiers: LCCN 2022055487 (print) | LCCN 2022055488 (ebook) | ISBN 9781984861184 (hardcover) | ISBN 9781984861191 (ebook)
Subjects: LCSH: Interior decoration. | Interior decorators—Anecdotes.
Classification: LCC NK2115 .G4233 2023 (print) | LCC NK2115 (ebook) | DDC 747—dc23/eng/20230105
LC record available at https://lccn.loc.gov/2022055487
LC ebook record available at https://lccn.loc.gov/2022055488

Hardcover ISBN: 978-1-9848-6118-4
eBook ISBN: 978-1-9848-6119-1

Printed in China

Acquiring editor: Dervla Kelley | Project editor: Kim Keller Production editor: Ashley Pierce | Editorial assistant: Gabby Urena | Designer and art director: Betsy Stromberg Production designers: Mari Gill and Faith Hague Production manager: Serena Sigona | Prepress color manager: Nick Patton | Copyeditor: Michelle Hubner Proofreader: Rita Madrigal | Marketer: Andrea Portanova

10 9 8 7 6 5 4 3 2 1

First Edition